# SPECTRUM®

# Reading

# Grade 7

Published by Spectrum®
an imprint of Carson-Dellosa Publishing LLC
Greensboro, NC 27425 USA

Spectrum®
An imprint of Carson-Dellosa Publishing LLC
P.O. Box 35665
Greensboro, NC 27425  USA

ISBN 978-1-4838-1220-5

03-087177811

# Table of Contents

# Cooking 101

*What is Kevin cooking up in class?*

1    Kevin felt as if he had stepped onto the set of *The Super Cookie Bake-Off* or one of the other dozen or so cooking competitions he loved watching so much. Two long, stainless steel tables sat in the middle of the kitchen, and a variety of ovens, sinks, refrigerators, and cupboards lined the walls. He expected a host to walk in, introduce everybody, and announce: "Today, our chefs must create a meal using only shiitake mushrooms, grape jelly, taco shells, and capers. You have 30 minutes, starting . . . now!"

2    Kevin smiled to himself, imagining the scene, and then looked around at the six other students in the class. Everyone was dressed in matching white chef's coats. Kevin began introducing himself to the student standing next to him, when Chef Mario suddenly burst through the door.

3    "Hello! Hello!" he greeted the class. "Welcome to Cooking 101. As I'm sure you read in the description, we'll be concentrating on a couple of simple dishes today. Once you've mastered those, we'll move onto something a bit more complex. So, who do we have with us for this session?"

4    One by one, each student shared his or her name, grade, and school. Then, Chef Mario passed out an egg to each student, along with some vegetables: green and red peppers, mushrooms, scallions, and black olives.

5    "We'll start with a basic omelet," explained Chef Mario. Kevin felt a bit disappointed. He had imagined whipping up a complicated meal, something that had a sauce and meat and a couple of side dishes. An omelet seemed too easy.

6    But then Chef Mario demonstrated his lighting-fast chopping skills. Next, he beat the egg into a frothy liquid with just a fork and some elbow grease. Then, he dumped the egg and vegetable mixture into a pan, added a few seasonings, and a few minutes later, the students were tasting a perfectly fluffy omelet.

7    When Kevin tried to imitate what the chef had done, he was surprised at how long the whole process took compared to how quickly the chef had worked. In the end, the omelets he and the others students made were flatter and less flavorful than Chef Mario's creation. Kevin had to admit it: his omelet had a lot of room for improvement.

8    Chef Mario explained why his omelet was fluffier, and he worked with the students as they attempted another omelet. With the chef's help, everyone's omelets were better the second time around, including Kevin's.

9    "Great work, everybody!" said the chef. "We've done breakfast, so let's try lunch now."

10    Chef Mario next showed the class how to make a turkey Reuben sandwich with coleslaw, Swiss cheese, Thousand Island dressing, and rye bread. He explained a couple of tricks that helped keep the coleslaw crispy and cool, while the turkey, cheese, and bread were piping hot.

11    "That contrast in temperature makes the sandwich extra special," he pointed out.

12    As with his omelet, Kevin's attempt at the Reuben was less than perfect, but he knew practice would make him better.

13    At the end of class, Chef Mario thanked everyone for coming. As he told the students that he looked forward to the next session, Kevin pictured himself at home on Saturday afternoon. He saw himself standing at the stove in his own kitchen, dressed in an apron, with his parents waiting at the table.

14    "Order up!" he would shout, and he'd set his culinary creations in front them. Perhaps the sandwiches wouldn't be perfect enough to win on a cooking show, but they would be perfectly delicious just the same.

NAME _____

1. Is this story fiction or nonfiction? Explain how you know.

   _fiction, it is not real_____

   _____

2. What two dishes were taught in the cooking class?

   _basic omlet_____        _turkey Reuben sandw_

3. How many students were in the class altogether? Place a checkmark on the line of the correct answer.

   _____ 7          _____ 11

   _____ 9          __✓__ This information is not in the story.

4. Which sentence below is a direct quote by Chef Mario from story? Place a checkmark on the line of the correct answer.

   __✓__ We'll start with a basic omelet.

   _____ My omelet was fluffier because I whipped it longer with a fork.

   _____ It's important to keep the coleslaw crisp and cool.

   _____ Thanks for coming!

5. Why do you think Kevin signed up for a cooking class? Cite evidence from the story to support your answer.

   _I think Evin signed up because he_____
   _wanted to become a chef._____

   _____

6. The author states that Kevin ". . . knew practice would make him better." Describe an experience of your own in which practice made you better at a particular skill.

   _When I started play sports, I would_____
   _ethier drop the ball or not catch it_____
   _but now I don't._____

# Julia Child

*How did an American-born woman become the French Chef?*

1   Julia McWilliams, who would later in life be known around the world as the French Chef Julia Child, was born in Pasadena, California, in 1912. She was an active, athletic young woman who played tennis, golf, and basketball, but cooking was not yet on her mind. She mostly aspired to be a writer, and so, when she graduated from Smith College in 1934, it was with a degree in English. Julia headed to New York City and began a career in advertising as a copywriter.

2   The attack on Pearl Harbor in 1941 brought the United States into World War II. Like many other Americans, Julia wanted to serve her country. She attempted to enlist in either the Army or the Navy, but her height of six feet two inches was deemed too tall for either service. Instead, Julia found a job with the Office of Strategic Services, or the OSS, known today as the CIA. She began as a typist, but she quickly rose in the ranks due to her intelligence and drive. Soon Julia was working as a top researcher, answering to General Donovan, head of the OSS.

3   Julia's assignments took her to China and other Asian nations. While stationed in Ceylon (now called *Sri Lanka*), she met another OSS employee, the man who would become her life-long best friend and husband: Paul Child. The two were married in 1946. Two years later, they moved to Paris, France, and Julia Child's culinary life began.

4   After eating at France's oldest restaurant, La Couronne, Julia had a revelation. She described the experience as "an opening up of the soul and spirit for me." She knew food and cooking were her passions, and she pursued her passion by enrolling in the world-famous Le Cordon Bleu cooking school. She also worked privately with master chefs and joined a women's cooking club.

5   Through the cooking club, Julia met two French women who were working to compile a master volume of French recipes. They hoped that Julia would be able to work with them to make the book appealing to Americans. With her experiences as a cook, an English major, and an American citizen, she seemed to be the perfect candidate.

6   The women worked together on the book for 10 years. Several times it was rejected for being too big or too much like an encyclopedia. But finally, in 1961, the massive, 726-page *Mastering the Art of French Cooking* was published in the United States. It seemed an unlikely candidate for popular success. However, the cookbook was critically acclaimed and topped the bestseller lists. French cooking swept the nation.

7   By then, Julia and Paul lived in Cambridge, Massachusetts. Based on the popularity of her book, Julia was invited to cook live on the air as a guest on a public television show in Boston. Her segment was so popular, the station decided to invite her back to host her own cooking show. Today, entire TV networks are dedicated to airing cooking and food-related programming. But in 1963, this idea was brand new. *The French Chef* debuted to immediate success, and the era of cooking shows was born.

8   Julia's show ran for the next 10 years. She continued writing, making public appearances, and, of course, cooking for the rest of her life. When Julia Child died in 2004, a couple of days shy of her 92nd birthday, she was arguably the most famous chef—French or otherwise—in the entire world.

**1.** Which genre of nonfiction best describes the text? Place a checkmark on the line of the correct answer.

_____ autobiography          _____ biography

___✓___ historical nonfiction          _____ essay

**2.** How did the author organize the information in the text? Do you think this was a good choice? Why or why not?

The athor explained her life in a couple of paragraphs. I this is was a good choice because it is much easier to read.

**3.** Reread the focus question below the title. Write a few sentences that answer the question, based on information from the text.

Julia had a job, USS/CIA. She traveled to different places. She moved to France, then the oldest resturant in France. She loved it!

**4.** Why did Julia Child and her co-writers have trouble publishing *Mastering the Art of French Cooking*?

it was to big or small

**5.** Which of the following statements is true? Place a checkmark on the line of the true statement.

_____ From the time she was young, Julia Child always dreamed of being a famous chef.

_____ Julia Child worked as a spy for the CIA during World War II.

_____ *Mastering the Art of French Cooking* was the book that inspired Julia Child to become a chef.

___✓___ Julia Child's first television show was called *The French Chef*.

**6.** What are you passionate about? How do you pursue your passions?

I am passionate on sports, I practice and play till I am great.

# Julia's Famous French Bread

*What steps will lead you to a delicious baguette?*

Equipment needed:

electric mixer with bowl, baking sheet, linen towel, baking stone, oven

Ingredients:

1 packet of instant yeast

$3\frac{1}{2}$ cups all-purpose flour

$2\frac{1}{4}$ teaspoons salt

$1\frac{1}{2}$ cups warm water (approximately 125°)

Preparation time: approximately 10 hours

Directions:

1. In a mixing bowl, combine the yeast, $2\frac{1}{2}$ cups of flour, and the salt. Using a flat beater in the electric mixer, mix the ingredients on low for about half a minute.

2. Continue mixing on low as you pour in the water.

3. After the dough has just begun to thicken, clean off the flat beater, and replace it with a dough hook. Mix in the remaining cup of flour, adding a little at a time until you have a soft, smooth dough that is a bit sticky. It should take about 5 minutes, and you may not need all the flour.

4. Remove the dough from the bowl and set it aside while you clean and dry the bowl.

5. Place the dough back in the bowl, and allow it to rise at room temperature for about 3 hours. When it has finished rising, the dough should be about 3–4 times its original size.

6. Using your fist, push down the dough into the bowl several times to deflate it. Then, reform the dough into a ball and place it back into the bowl. Let the dough rise again at room temperature for a couple of hours. When the dough is ready, it will be about $2\frac{1}{2}$–3 times the original size.

7. While the dough is rising, place a linen towel onto a baking sheet, and rub flour into the towel's fabric.

8. Once the dough has finished rising for the second time, divide it into several equal pieces, depending on how large you want your finished loaves to be. Shape each loaf, and place all of them on the towel-covered baking sheet. Loosely cover the loaves and let them rise for a third time, for approximately 2 hours.

9. Preheat your oven to 450°. Place a baking stone on the center rack and allow it to heat with the oven.

10. Once the loaves have finished rising for the last time, slash each loaf diagonally across the top 2 or 3 times. Spray the loaves with water. Then, place the loaves onto the preheated baking stone.

11. Bake the loaves for about 25 minutes, or until they are golden brown. While they are baking, spray the loaves lightly with water 3 times at approximately 5-minute intervals.

12. Allow the loaves to cool for a couple of hours before you try to cut them.

13. Enjoy your delicious baguettes!

**1.** Identify the author's main purpose for writing the text. Place a checkmark on the line of the correct answer.

_____ entertain          _____ inform

_____ convince          _____ explain

**2.** How does the text's organizational structure support the author's purpose?

_____

_____

_____

**3.** Why do you think the ingredients list is placed near the beginning of the text rather than near the end?

_____

_____

**4.** Approximately how much time does the dough need to rise in total? Place a checkmark on the line of the correct answer.

_____ 3 hours          _____ 7 hours

_____ 5 hours          _____ 10 hours

**5.** Which step occurs immediately after the third and final rising of the dough? Place a checkmark on the line of the correct answer.

_____ Shape the dough into loaves.          _____ Place the loaves into the oven.

_____ Slash the loaves diagonally.          _____ Spray the loaves with water.

**6.** Describe a time when you followed steps to complete a process. Were the steps clearly described? Was the end result a success?

_____

_____

_____

_____

# Take a Hike, Allergies!

*What food allergies are most common and what happens when people consume food they are allergic to?*

1  As Georgia's scout troop gathers to plan their meals for the upcoming hike through Pennsylvania, Jessica yells excitedly, "Of course we'll need trail mix!"

2  The other girls laugh, but Georgia groans inwardly. She knows she has to once again educate her friends about her peanut allergy. Having a severe allergic reaction on the trail—in the middle of nowhere—would be a catastrophe.

3  Luckily, their scout leader, Michelle, is prepared to negotiate the issue. "Trail mix sounds like a great idea, but we'll have to be careful to keep everyone in mind as we're planning our meals. Georgia is allergic to peanuts, and Angela is allergic to eggs."

4  Georgia's head snaps up to look at Angela. She didn't know another girl in their troop had allergies.

5  "Yeah, sorry," says Angela. "I don't mean to cause problems, but when I eat eggs, I have serious physical reactions. My mouth and lips swell right away. I can actually go into anaphylaxis, which means I have trouble breathing because my throat swells up, my blood pressure drops, and I might even pass out. Eggs make me feel really sick to my stomach, too."

6  Michelle adds, "We'll definitely leave eggs and peanuts off the menu, but we'll have to be very careful about the ingredients in all the foods we take with us. Sometimes foods have eggs or peanuts listed as ingredients, and you never would have guessed they would be in there."

7  "For me," explains Georgia, "it's always best if a product notes right on the packaging that it was made in a peanut-free facility. Even the tiniest trace of peanuts immediately stuffs up my nose and makes it hard for me to breathe, and I start wheezing. My body also swells, and I get covered with big raised bumps called *hives*. I *really* don't want this to happen to me when we are a day's hike away from the nearest town."

8  "So, this will be a challenge," Jessica says thoughtfully, "but we can do it. Let's get started on our menus! I wish I knew more about food allergies now, though."

9  "I've been reading about allergies," replies Michelle. "An allergic reaction happens because the body thinks certain foods are trying to harm it. The most common allergens are eggs, fish, milk, tree nuts, peanuts, shellfish, soy, and wheat. Most allergens are proteins. Let's get our menu finished, and then we can talk some more about food allergies. This is an important conversation, because we have to be prepared to handle any emergency we encounter on the trail. Allergic reactions are definitely among these emergencies that could come up."

10  Jessica whips out a pen. Poised to write, she asks the girls, "What would you like in your trail mix, then?"

11  "Definitely not peanuts. Or hard-boiled eggs," Rachel declares and giggles at the thought of hard-boiled eggs in their trail mix. Georgia breathes a huge sigh of relief, because her friends are happily embracing the challenge to make sure everyone stays healthy on their hike. Now that she doesn't have to worry about annoying everyone in her troop, her mind turns to wondering if her friends might like cranberries in their trail mix, like she does.

12  After the menus are finally completed, Erin, who is usually the quietest in the group, begins bouncing excitedly in her seat. "You know," she says, "we came up with a much better menu than we would have if you guys didn't have allergies. We are going to have an amazing time and eat some amazing food, too!"

13  Everyone smiles as they nod their heads in agreement.

**1.** Sometimes authors have more than one purpose for writing a text. Did this text have more than one purpose? Explain your answer.

The porpose of this story is to tell you about food alergys.

**2.** What was Georgia allergic to? Place a checkmark on the line of the correct answer.

_____ cranberries  ✓ peanuts

_____ eggs  _____ milk

**3.** What is *anaphylaxis*? Use context clues from the text for your answer.

Anaphylaxis is a alergic reation that causes mout and lips to swell up.

**4.** What is the conflict in this story? How is it resolved?

The conflict is when Georgia goss on a hike but she is alergic to all the foods on the manue. It is resolved becaus she and Erin told the leaders, thens the changed the menue.

**5.** Who is Michelle? Place a checkmark on the line of the correct answer.

_____ Georgia's best friend  ✓ scout leader

_____ the girl who is allergic to eggs  _____ Angela's mother

**6.** What steps could you take to help a friend or classmate with a severe food allergy stay healthy and safe?

Make sure that nothing they eat has what they are allergic to. And also make them not have to eat beea se of their alergy and give them some,

# Let's Move

*How does the First Lady's fitness and nutrition plan encourage children to take responsibility for their own good health?*

1     What were you doing at 4:30 or 5:00 this morning? As most people slept, Michelle Obama was probably starting her daily workout and waiting for her husband, President Barack Obama, to join her. Michelle Obama prefers to begin each day with exercise. Many First Ladies over the years picked a particular cause or two to promote while in the White House. Lady Bird Johnson led beautification campaigns, saying that "where flowers bloom, so does hope." Barbara Bush led a push for literacy, encouraging families to read to their children. In 2010, Michelle Obama launched a campaign that fit well with her interests in a healthy lifestyle: Let's Move!

2     The goal of Let's Move is "solving the challenge of childhood obesity within a generation." In the United States, one in five children of school age is obese. One child in three is overweight. Contributors to this epidemic include sugary snacks, larger portions, and time spent sitting in front of electronic devices. At an event in Miami, Florida, Mrs. Obama noted, "Everybody here knows that kids who eat well and stay active tend to have better grades. They have better attendance. They have fewer disciplinary problems at school."

3     The program encourages children to take five actions steps. They are:

    1. Move every day
    2. Try new fruits and vegetables
    3. Drink lots of water
    4. Do jumping jacks to break up TV time
    5. Help make dinner.

4     The campaign requires children to be active for 60 minutes each day. This can happen on playgrounds, in parks, in school, and at home with their families. The 60 minutes of activity doesn't have to happen all at one time. If children are watching TV or playing a computer game, they should take breaks. During these breaks, they can do some jumping jacks, push-ups, or run up and down stairs. They can walk around the block after supper with their families. Some families even assign activities during ads. For example, everyone must do ten sit-ups, ten push-ups, and ten jumping jacks before sitting down to watch the end of a program. Young people can earn achievement awards for being active, such as the Presidential Active Lifestyle Award.

5     Mrs. Obama has worked with families, schools, and community leaders to encourage children to pursue outside activities. She has also encouraged the development of recreational areas. As part of Let's Move, the First Lady made appearances on TV comedy shows and news programs. She posted videos online and asked Americans to show how they are being active. She shared healthy recipes on social media sites. Many people used the hash tag #LetsMove, including the President and Vice President!

6     Let's Move helps children learn to think about what they eat. It helps them actively plan meals and budget for shopping. They buy food that is healthier than what they might normally choose. And some children even grow their own food! They plant their own gardens to ensure that they have fresh vegetables ready right at home. Instead of salty or sugary high-calorie foods, they are urged to have a fruit or vegetable with every snack or meal. They learn to add variety by trying new foods and new combinations of foods, such as smoothies. Children are most likely to be successful if they plan meals with their families, choose their own ingredients, and discover exciting new recipes. As they make their own choices, they become more likely to be successful.

**1.** Who started the Let's Move campaign? _____

**2.** Which of the following is NOT one the five action steps for Let's Move? Place a checkmark on the line of the correct answer.

_____ Drink lots of water.                    _____ Try new fruits and vegetables.

_____ Plant a garden.                         _____ Help make dinner.

**3.** List three ways Michelle Obama promoted the Let's Move campaign.

1. _____

2. _____

3. _____

**4.** Write a sentence describing the main idea of the selection.

_____

_____

**5.** Does the author have a positive or negative point of view about the Let's Move campaign? How do you know?

_____

_____

_____

_____

**6.** What evidence does the author cite to support the idea that the Let's Move campaign is important?

_____

_____

_____

**7.** Do you think the Let's Move campaign is having a positive affect on American children? Why or why not?

_____

_____

_____

_____

# The Future of Food Today

*What kinds of foods exist where technology and creativity intersect?*

1    In the world of science fiction, an astronaut or other space traveler might get a complete meal in pill form. They might punch a few buttons on a machine and, a few seconds later, have a freshly made five-course dinner appear before them. And in some darker science fiction stories, earthlings themselves might end up being dinner! But what is the reality of high-tech food? It's not as far from those science fiction ideas as you might think.

2    At the Massachusetts Institute of Technology (MIT), scientists have developed a 3-D food printer. Instead of holding ink tanks, this printer works using food canisters that eject ingredients. To make a meal, the "cook" first loads the printer with the canisters he or she needs for a specific recipe. With the push of a few buttons, the printer goes to work mixing the ingredients. Then, it either heats or cools them to a precisely determined temperature, and *voila!* A ready-made meal, with no waste and little effort, is the end result.

3    Nearby, at Harvard University, researchers are working on an idea that could help reduce the amount of plastic packaging that ends up as garbage. Imagine finishing a bottle of water, but instead of looking for a recycling container to toss the plastic container in, you simply eat it. A new, plastic-like substance has been developed that is completely edible. Similar in feel to the skin of a grape, the substance can be formed into a thin membrane, which can enclose foods and drinks the same way plastic has for decades. The difference is, the membrane can be flavored to taste like whatever it holds. And you don't have to throw it away—it's just one more part of the taste experience!

4    In addition to the waste created by our pre-packaged food culture, some people also object to the way animals are treated. What if, instead of slaughtering animals for meat, we could grow meat like we grow vegetables? It may be hard to believe, but we can. Richard Hederstierna has designed a special kind of "cooker," called the *Cocoon*, that uses animal or fish cells to grow meat. When a packet of specific animal cells are placed inside the Cocoon, it heats them for a certain amount of time. The cells reproduce and form a piece of meat or fish, depending on which kind of animal cells you placed in the machine. Some people believe this device can also help address food shortages in parts of the world.

5    Another change in the way we use animal products is the creation of an artificial egg product. Eggs have always played a vital role in cooking. They help baked goods rise. They bind together ingredients in spreads, sauces, and other dishes. Eggs are high in nutrition, and most people enjoy their taste. It was long thought impossible that another food could replicate the versatility of an egg. However, after years of searching and experimenting, several plants have been discovered that can be used instead. Vegans, or people who do not eat or use any animal products whatsoever, can now enjoy eggless cookies or mayonnaise that tastes no different than ones made with chicken eggs.

6    Someday, all these future foods may seem completely common to us. There was a time when frozen food was a futuristic marvel. Today, you pass the freezer section at the grocery store without giving it much thought. Perhaps in 20 years, everybody will make breakfast by creating omelets on 3-D printers and frying up sausages that grew in containers on their counters.

**1.** List the four examples of high-tech foods discussed in the text.

_____

_____

_____

_____

**2.** Complete the analogy.

*Ink tanks* are to *traditional printers* as _____ are to *3-D food printers.*

**3.** What example does the author provide of a food technology that is common to us today, but that was once viewed as futuristic? Place a checkmark on the line of the correct answer.

_____ eggs                    _____ 3-D food printer

_____ frozen food           _____ bottled water

**4.** Write one fact presented in the text.

_____

**5.** Write one opinion presented in the text.

_____

_____

**6.** Does the author provide a balanced and unbiased point of view about the future foods covered in the text? Explain your answer.

_____

_____

_____

**7.** Imagine a future food technology that has not been developed. Write a few sentences describing what you imagine. How does this technology benefit people?

_____

_____

_____

_____

# Welcome to the Days of Olde

*What do Madison and her family see at the Renaissance Fair?*

1    "Hear, ye! Hear ye! All bow for King Frederick and Queen Vanessa!"

2    The bearded man yelling these words wore a white shirt with puffy sleeves under a tan vest, along with loose pants that gathered tightly at his ankles. Behind him, King Frederick and Queen Vanessa strolled slowly, waving to the crowds that parted and bowed for them. The King's long robe brushed the ground as he walked, and the Queen had huge, ruffled sleeves on her dress, an elaborate hairpiece atop her head, and several long, beaded necklaces draping down her front.

3    They were the King and Queen of the Renaissance Fair, but like most people, they had regular jobs they went to when they weren't playing royalty at the fair. Each year, all the people who worked or volunteered at the annual Renaissance Fair cast votes to decide who would be that year's King and Queen. Usually, a couple who had participated in the fair for many years was chosen.

4    Madison hoped someday she could work at the fair, and maybe even be Queen one day. She and her family had been attending the annual event for the last few years. Madison loved all the pretending, especially the way the people in costumes spoke using very old-fashioned English, like they were in one of Shakespeare's plays.

5    The buildings lining the main avenue of the fair were built to look like the shops and inns of a medieval village. The insides of the shops were more modern, with cash registers and credit card machines, but the goods on sale were Renaissance-themed items. One store had plastic battle axes, long swords, and other pretend weapons for sale. Another shop sold light, flowing clothes, flowered crowns, and jeweled tiaras. Craftspeople displayed their wares through the fair. They included wood carvers, metal smiths, and weavers.

6    As Madison and her family wandered through the festival, they saw jugglers, fire eaters, and a lot of men dressed as knights. A rope was strung tightly between two trees, and a man walked carefully back and forth, balancing a woman on his shoulders. Madison's brother suddenly ran ahead and got in line at a food stand. He was ready to get their traditional Renaissance Fair lunch: a roasted turkey leg. Madison and her parents joined him, and with foil-wrapped turkey legs in hand, the family soon continued on their way through the festival.

7    They passed a manual merry-go-round offering rides for a couple of dollars. Four men worked at the center of the ride to keep it spinning. Handles stuck out that they grabbed onto and pushed as they ran around and around, making the merry-go-round go faster and faster. Madison had ridden it last year, but all the spinning had made her feel dizzy, so she decided to skip the ride this time.

8    The long avenue ended at the jousting field. Several times a day, jousters competed there. Riding horses and wielding long lances, the jousters tried to knock each other off their horses. It was one of the most popular events at the fair, and the stands surrounding the field were usually packed. The family arrived just in time to grab a few of the last seats.

9    The King and Queen sat in a special building at the far end of the field, and as the riders came out, each one stopped to pay his respects. Then, the horses carried their riders to opposite ends of the field, where they waited to begin. All at once, the riders started racing toward each other with the lances pointed straight ahead. One knight had a better angle, and he knocked his opponent to the ground. The crowd cheered.

10    As Madison walked with her family back through the fair, they stopped in a shop selling Renaissance costumes. Madison picked out the outfit she would wear next year. It would be her first time dressing up, and she couldn't wait.

1. Which of the following is NOT included in the story as something Madison and her family saw at the Renaissance Fair?

_____ a group of medieval singers          _____ a tightrope walker

_____ a fire eater          _____ fake weapons

2. Besides cash registers and credit card machines, list three other kinds of modern equipment that would most likely be part of a Renaissance Fair.

_____

_____

_____

3. Explain what *jousting* is.

_____

_____

4. Why does Madison choose not to ride on the merry-go-round?

_____

5. In your own words, describe the meaning of *manual* based on how the word is used to describe the merry-go-round.

_____

_____

6. Why do you think the King and Queen are often a couple who have been part of the fair for many years? Explain your answer.

_____

_____

_____

7. The people at a Renaissance Fair dress up and reenact what life might have been like in medieval times. If you could choose a different time period to have people reenact, what would it be? Describe details of what would be included in the reenactment, including what people might wear or do.

_____

_____

_____

_____

# Maria Merian: Artist, Naturalist

*How do Maria Merian's skills and passions help her succeed?*

1    Centuries ago, at a time when most women had little independence or power over their lives, Maria Merian used her artistic skills and knowledge of the natural world to achieve great success. Merian's patience and keen sense of observation allowed her to see things in the insect world that other scientists were missing. Metamorphosis, or the way caterpillars change into butterflies and moths, was the main focus of her life's work. However, her beautiful paintings and drawings depicted a wide range of insects and other wildlife.

2    Born in Germany in 1647, Merian's artistic skills were developed at a young age. Her birthfather died when she was just three years old, but her mother remarried quickly. Merian's new stepfather was an accomplished still life painter. He began right away to share his skills with Merian. As her talents grew, so did her interest in insects. Merian was known for capturing caterpillars and bringing them home. Then, she would closely observe the way they spun cocoons and transformed into butterflies or moths. When Merian was thirteen, the insects became the main subjects of her paintings.

3    In the 1600s, metamorphosis was not well understood, even by the world's greatest scientists. Merian's careful studies and her depictions of each step of the process went beyond what anyone else was doing at the time.

4    While still a teen, Merian married and moved to a new town. The focus of her art switched to flowers growing locally. Soon, she published her first book of paintings: *The Book of Flowers.* However, it was not long before she returned to bugs. Her second book featured studies of insect life.

5    Merian continued painting, but she also became the mother of two children. Then, after 14 years of marriage, she and her husband separated. Divorce was not common in the 1690s, but it did occur. On her own and with two children, Merian made a move that would change her life. She headed to the thriving metropolis of Amsterdam, Netherlands. For a single woman, the city was a good choice.

Women had more rights there than they did in many other places. Women could own property and businesses. Before long, Merian had her own studio where she painted still lives of flowers, birds, and bugs and sold them to the public. Her business was very successful.

6    Success meant that Merian was too busy to spend time as a naturalist studying the lives of insects. She missed that work greatly. In her 50s, she decided to use her profits to travel to one of the Netherlands' territories, the South American nation of Suriname. So far, Merian had observed insects mostly in the groomed gardens of Europe. Now, she would have a chance to see insects in an entirely wild and natural habitat: the jungles of Suriname.

7    In the hot and humid South American forests, Merian found giant moths with wingspans a foot wide, spiders big enough to eat small birds, and brightly colored lizards. When she finally returned to Holland, she was ready to publish a new volume of her work. The lively paintings captured the South American insects, birds, and plants in action, and they often showed different life stages of a specimen within a single image. Entitled *The Insects of Suriname,* the book sold well, but many scientists of the time criticized it. They claimed that much of what she had painted was untrue. These criticisms largely came from the scientists' ignorance. They simply did not believe that what Merian depicted could be real. Her reputation as a naturalist suffered because of these critics.

8    Merian died in 1717. Shortly afterward, a final volume of her work was published by her daughter. In the 20th century, her work was rediscovered. Much more is known about the natural world now, and Merian's studies are appreciated for being well ahead of their time. Today, Maria Merian is recognized as a groundbreaking artist and naturalist.

**1.** Classify the following statements by writing **O** if the statement is an opinion, or **F** if the statement is a fact.

_____ Merian's stepfather created beautiful still lives.

_____ Amsterdam, Netherlands, was the best city Merian could have chosen to move to.

_____ The hot and humid jungles of Suriname provided many different kinds of insects for Merian to observe.

_____ The most important event in Merian's life was traveling to Suriname.

_____ The main focus of much of Merian's work was studying the process of metamorphosis.

_____ After being somewhat forgotten for many centuries, the work of Maria Merian was rediscovered during the 20ᵗʰ century.

**2.** What is *metamorphosis*?

_____

**3.** What made Amsterdam a good place for Merian to move to?

_____

_____

**4.** Identify the sentence in the first paragraph that presents the main idea of the text. Write the sentence below.

_____

_____

**5.** Does the author present sufficient evidence and details in the text to support the main idea? Explain your answer.

_____

_____

_____

**6.** Do you think Merian's gender played a role in the scientists' criticisms of her work? Why or why not?

_____

_____

_____

# A Feast Fit for a King

*What did Europeans of the Middle Ages eat?*

1    Imagine a medieval feast. What do you see? Is King Henry XIII clutching a giant turkey leg in one hand and a shiny goblet in the other? Is everyone around him eating with their hands, making a mess, as servants pile platter after platter of meat onto an elaborately decorated table? Although this is a fun image, it is only partially true.

2    People in the Middle Ages did eat with their hands. Personal utensils were mostly unheard of, especially forks. There were spoons to help serve, but only special guests would receive a knife from the host. Everyone else would be expected to bring their own. Of course, eating with one's hands can be quite a sticky or greasy situation, so towels were provided to help diners stay at least somewhat clean as they ate.

3    Still, dining was often a messy affair. At special occasions in the wealthiest households, women tended to dine alone, separate from the men. Women were expected to uphold an aura of grace and refinement. Eating greasy meat by hand would certainly undermine that goal! Once the men and women had finished their meals, they would come together to socialize.

4    Dietary scholars of the Middle Ages believed that the foods in a meal needed to be served and eaten in order of heaviness. The lightest and most easily digested foods, such as fruits and cheeses, were eaten first to help the digestive system get started. Once digestion was underway, greens and light meats, such as lettuce, cabbage, and chicken, could be eaten. Last came the heavier vegetables and meats, such as carrots, beans, beef, pork, and mutton. This method was considered the most healthful way to eat.

5    The main and largest meal of the day was supper, and it was eaten at midday. Dinner was a light meal, and many of those in nobility—the highest levels of medieval society—skipped breakfast altogether. Breakfast was considered unnecessary and indulgent for those who did not perform manual labor. Snacks and any other eating during the day were viewed the same way. Commoners, or the working class, were allowed to eat breakfast and small meals throughout the day.

6    Most of what people ate during medieval times was grown or raised locally. Transportation of goods was slow and expensive, so only the wealthiest could afford exotic foods and spices. But those at the highest economic levels enjoyed spicing and flavoring their foods. Black pepper, ginger, and saffron were common spices imported to enhance European cuisine.

7    People at the lower level of society ate quite differently. The idea of class structure dictated which foods were available to those in different economic levels, so working class families tended to eat less-refined meals. They certainly did not use spices, and even beef was too expensive. However, grains were widely available, and bread was the most common food eaten by all. Many meals involved *sops,* which were small pieces of bread used to sop up a liquid, such as broth or a sauce.

8    As the Middle Ages continued, a middle class of merchants and craftspeople emerged. They strove to imitate the wealthiest members of Medieval society, including the dining habits of those in higher social classes. So rules were put in place that stated what kinds of foods a person was allowed to eat, based on social status.

9    Today, we have a lot of freedom about what, when, and how we eat. During your next meal, try to imagine how different your dining experience would be if you were eating during the Middle Ages.

**I.** What was the most common food in Medieval Europe? Place a checkmark on the line of the correct answer.

_____ beef                        _____ bread

_____ chicken                   _____ broth

**2.** Why were spices a luxury?

_____

**3.** Why were towels provided during medieval feasts?

_____

_____

**4.** Complete the following statement.

Noblewomen often ate separately from men because _____

_____

**5.** Why did nobility avoid eating breakfast?

_____

_____

**6.** Which of the following was NOT a detail described in the text? Place a checkmark on the line of the correct answer.

_____ A middle class emerged during the Middle Ages.

_____ What people ate was largely determined by their economic level in society.

_____ For the most part, clergy and nobility were allowed to eat the same types of foods.

_____ Different kinds of foods were eaten in specific order to help with digestion.

**7.** Think about the last meal you ate, including the food, the setting, and the etiquette. How was it similar to and different from a meal during the Middle Ages?

_____

_____

_____

_____

_____

# Take a Bow

*Have you ever tried to learn a new skill?*

1   Each year, Dan and I attend our town's annual Medieval Festival, because I appreciate learning about life in ancient times. Today, the sun is blazing, and although I crave the cool shade of the large tents nearby, my gaze is fixed on the men and women a short distance away who are rapidly firing arrows. One of the festival ambassadors notices my gaping jaw and asks me if I'd like to learn a little more about archery.

2   "Absolutely!" I reply too loudly, but I can't contain my enthusiasm.

3   "There's a free lesson today at 3:00, if you're interested," says the ambassador. "It will be offered where the actors are demonstrating right now."

4   "This is amazing, of course we'll go!" I assert, and Dan nods his head in agreement.

5   After rehydrating in one of the tents before the lesson begins, we wander toward the archery range and witness a small crowd gathering around a young woman with a bow in her hand.

6   "If you're here for archery instruction, we're about to get started," she says. "I'm Megan. You might have seen me earlier demonstrating my skill while dressed in a medieval costume. Archery is an ancient sport, and believe it or not, for a short time it was actually the only sport allowed in England. The monarchy at the time knew archers were necessary to defend the British Isles against enemy invaders. I am assuming, though, that you didn't come here for a history lesson. Who's excited to commence fire?"

7   "Me!" yells the entire assembly in chorus.

8   Megan hands an armguard to each member of the group. "Put this snugly on your arm to protect yourself from getting whacked with the bowstring." After we adjust the guards on our arms, Megan walks among the group once more, handing each participant a single arrow and a bow. "Please keep your arrows down and off the bowstring until it's your turn. We are going to take turns shooting at a target."

9   Behind her is a single large bull's-eye target, and I want nothing more than to sink my arrow right into its yellow center. Megan senses my eagerness. "Would you like to go first?" she asks. I nod enthusiastically, and she instructs me to grip the bowstring with my three inner fingers and level the bow. She helps me snap the nock (the end of the arrow) into the bowstring and encourages me to launch the arrow when I feel comfortable.

10   I hesitate before pulling back on the string, and this causes the arrow to plummet to the ground. No one in the group laughs, though, because it takes a lot of effort to pull back the bowstring. Megan assists as I arm my bow for the second time, and when I feel my aim is perfectly aligned with the target's center, I relax my string fingers, and the arrow shoots off toward the target. While the arrow doesn't pierce the yellow center of the bull's-eye, I am thrilled because it does hit the blue ring of the target's perimeter.

11   "Amazing job!" Megan compliments. She assesses the activity on the range and announces, "Clear!" so everyone knows there is no one currently shooting. She encourages Dan to take a picture of me and the arrow in the target

12   "Ready, Brandon?" Dan asks, and then he takes my picture.

13   Dan gets to have his turn to shoot next, and he completely misses the target. But he doesn't mind at all. We're both so excited about archery, we decide to take additional lessons. Megan gives us a pamphlet about the archery academy. If we do well, we will participate as actors in next year's Medieval Festival to demonstrate our new skill!

**1.** Which point of view is used in telling this story: first-person, second-person, or third-person? Explain how you know.

_____

_____

_____

**2.** Identify the order of events in the story by writing 1–8 on the lines.

_____ Dan and Brandon get a drink of water.

_____ Megan gives Dan and Brandon a pamphlet about archery lessons.

_____ Dan misses the target.

_____ Megan shares a little bit about the history of archery.

_____ Brandon hits the edge of the target with his arrow.

_____ Dan and Brandon see men and women shooting arrows.

_____ Brandon drops his arrow.

_____ Dan and Brandon attend a Medieval Festival.

**3.** What is the story's setting?

place: _____     time: _____

**4.** Although Dan misses the target when he tried to shoot an arrow, he decides to take archery classes with Brandon. What does this tell you about Dan?

_____

_____

_____

**5.** Describe a time when you failed at a new skill. How did you feel? Did you try to get better?

_____

_____

_____

_____

_____

# Keeper of the Castle

*What does Brandon learn about the structure of a castle?*

1   The English countryside unrolled in all directions, dotted here and there with a few trees. At first the view had seemed quite pretty, but after three hours in the car watching the green roll by, Brandon was pretty bored. But suddenly, as they rounded a sharp curve, the stone towers of Berylbridge Castle peaked above the distant hills, and he sat up with excitement.

2   "Do you guys see it?" Brandon exclaimed, pointing to the ancient gray building rising above the horizon.

3   "Finally," Mr. and Mrs. Mackey said in unison. They were ready to get out of the car as well.

4   After parking and paying the entrance fee, Brandon and his parents followed the path leading up to the castle's front. As they neared the building, Brandon saw the entire structure was encircled by a moat, and the only way across the water was a small bridge at the end of the path. A group of other visitors, as well as a tour guide, were gathered on the bridge.

5   As the Mackeys joined the group, the tour guide announced, "Now that everyone is here, let's get started. Welcome to Berylbridge Castle. It has stood here, solid as stone, for nearly 750 years. Like most castles, this one was built to protect those living inside from a military attack. The first line of defense is what you see here in front of you: the moat."

6   The guide explained that the moat made it difficult to get anywhere near the walls of the castle. "It was not always filled with water," he added, "but a deep ditch with steep sides served the same purpose. As attackers struggled to cross it, the archers positioned up there along the walls and in the towers would have an easy opportunity for shooting."

7   The group crossed the small bridge, which was the only way into the castle. The guide pointed out the large chains that could be used to raise the bridge and seal up the entrance to the castle. "With the drawbridge raised, the castle becomes extremely secure."

8   As the tour passed through the gatehouse and entered the open courtyard inside the castle, Brandon learned that the exterior walls were up to 12 feet thick in many places. Attackers had almost no chance of breaking through such solid stone structures. The guide added, "Some parts of the walls are even wider and have rooms inside them that are used for the kitchen, storage, sleeping quarters, and other purposes."

9   The guide pointed out other, smaller buildings within the courtyard. One building was used for stables, and another was a chapel. Lining the insides of the castle walls were many doors leading to small rooms. These were mostly rooms for the dozens of families that lived and worked inside the castle. At the very back corner of the courtyard stood a large stone building, taller even than the towers at each corner of the castle.

10   "That building," the guide told the group, "is the *keep*. The keep is the most secure area, almost like a castle within the castle. The noble family that owned and ruled the castle and the surrounding land lived inside the keep, and if attackers did get inside the castle walls, everyone retreated to there."

11   After the tour ended, Brandon and his parents climbed a winding, stone staircase to the top of the front tower and looked through the tall, thin windows at the surrounding fields. The view inspired Brandon to imagine armored knights on horseback charging across the green to attack the castle, and he was a proud nobleman getting ready to defend his home and his people . . .

12   But the view also included the parking lot—and the car he'd be spending another three hours sitting in—and Brandon's immediate future looked a little less exciting.

**I.** Who is the main character of this story? Place a checkmark on the line of the correct answer.

_____ Berylbridge Castle          _____ Brandon Mackey

_____ Mr. Mackey                  _____ the tour guide

**2.** Explain the purpose of a drawbridge.

_____

_____

_____

**3.** According to the text, how does a moat help protect a castle?

_____

_____

_____

**4.** What is this text mostly about?

_____ Brandon's feelings about the car ride     _____ the purpose and structure of castles

_____ Brandon's enjoyment of the tour           _____ the purpose of the keep

**5.** How would this text have been different if it were nonfiction explanatory text?

_____

_____

_____

_____

**6.** Have you taken a tour of a historical site or other kind of place? Write a short paragraph comparing the tour you took with the tour Brandon takes in the story.

_____

_____

_____

_____

# Jim Abbott Fails to Quit

*How did Jim Abbott overcome a physical challenge to become a successful pitcher in baseball's Major Leagues?*

1    When you learn that Jim Abbott went to the college baseball World Series, played in the Olympics, and pitched a no-hitter, it might come as a surprise to hear that Abbott was also born without a fully formed right hand. How did a man with only one good hand become so successful in a sport that normally requires two?

2    During his youth, Abbott's parents did not give him particularly special treatment, but they did send him off to school every day with encouraging phrases, such as "Be a leader." When he was in kindergarten, Abbott was given a sock with a metal pincher on the end to wear on his right hand, but neither he nor his family thought the benefit of this device was worth the frustrations it caused. For one thing, his arm became sweaty and it was very uncomfortable to wear. Abbott decided not to wear any kind of prosthetic aid.

3    Abbot did not always like that his right hand had not formed correctly, but he took it as a challenge. Perhaps life wasn't easy or fair, but he decided to make the best of it and find his own way of doing things. As long he could play sports, he figured, everything else would be all right, so he worked at becoming a highly competitive athlete. Abbott enjoyed all sports, and he played baseball, basketball, and football while in high school. None of it was easy. He was cut from the freshman basketball team, and after he made the freshman baseball team, he went an entire season without a hit. But despite these setbacks, he never quit trying.

4    By the time Abbott went to college, he could throw a baseball almost 90 miles per hour. His team, the Michigan Wolverines, won two league championships while he was pitching for them. In 1988, the California Angels signed Abbott to a major-league baseball contract, but before he joined his team, he went to the Olympic Games in Seoul, South Korea. Abbott played on the United States' gold-medal winning baseball team there.

5    When Jim Abbott began playing for the California Angels, opposing players thought he would have difficulty fielding the ball. He couldn't use two hands at the same time, so batters tried bunting the ball, hitting it directly at him because they figured he would not be able to field it. This tactic was futile. When Abbott pitched, he slipped a mitt onto his right forearm. Then, as soon as his pitch was launched, he would put the mitt on his left hand quickly enough to field the ball. He would then place the mitt between his body and right arm, grab the ball, and throw out the runner at first.

6    After four seasons with the California Angels, Abbott was traded to the New York Yankees. He was frustrated that he was not playing well, but true to his spirit, he wasn't about to give up. Instead, he continued playing with determination, and in 1993, he pitched a no-hitter for the Yankees. The opposing team, the Cleveland Indians, got no hits and scored only one run. A no-hit game is a rare event in baseball, with an average of only two games or so per year that are no-hitters. Abbott continued playing until 1999, when he retired.

7    In addition to his baseball skills, Jim Abbott is known for his kindness. He continues to contribute to the development of students and young athletes. He still lives in California and helps young pitchers during the Angels' spring training sessions. Throughout his life, whenever he felt sorry for himself, he became immediately ashamed. He refused to quit trying because of the people who loved him, but most importantly, he refused to quit trying for himself. Abbott now greatly appreciates his individuality.

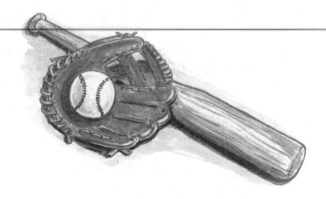

**1.** Why might some people find it surprising that Jim Abbott was a successful professional baseball player?

_____

**2.** Why did Jim Abbott choose not to use a prosthetic hand?

_____

_____

**3.** Which of the following is NOT a team Jim Abbott played with? Place a checkmark on the line of the correct answer.

_____ Michigan Wolverines          _____ Cleveland Indians

_____ California Angels            _____ New York Yankees

**4.** In your own words, explain how Jim Abbott was able to pitch, catch, and throw using only one hand.

_____

_____

_____

_____

_____

**5.** The author believes that Jim Abbott was a successful baseball player. What evidence does the author cite to support this idea? Do you agree with the author? Why or why not?

_____

_____

_____

_____

_____

**6.** Despite physical challenges that could be frustrating at times, Jim Abbott refused to feel sorry for himself and never quit trying his best to succeed. Write a description of someone you know who shares one or both of these attributes.

_____

_____

_____

# The Black Sox Scandal

*What would motivate some of baseball's greatest players to cheat?*

1   Although sports scandals have become somewhat common news items these days, that was not the case a hundred years ago. When the public learned that players on the 1919 Chicago White Sox baseball team tried to lose games on purpose, it rocked the sports world. Known as the Black Sox Scandal, it remains today as one of the most famous sports scandals in history.

2   In 1919, the Chicago White Sox were considered the greatest baseball team of the time. They were headed to the World Series, where they would play nine games against the Cincinnati Reds.

3   Despite their success, the White Sox players were unhappy men. They may have been among the greatest players of the time, but they were also among the worst paid. Even within the team, there was disparity in how much each player earned. Some players were paid more than twice what others earned, and this created further friction and unhappiness within the team.

4   So why didn't the players just quit and go play for other teams? At that time, players could not easily move to a new team. According to the contracts players signed, they had to get the permission of their current team's owner in order to move to another team. Of course, an owner would be reluctant to allow a great player to leave his team, and White Sox owner Charles Comiskey was no exception. He would not let anyone go, but at the same time, he refused to pay his great players what they were worth.

5   We now have two elements that led to the Black Sox Scandal—disgruntled players and a greedy owner—but the third element is the most important: gambling. Tremendous amounts of money were won or lost based on the outcomes of baseball games. Several gamblers, working together, approached a group of White Sox players and offered them $100,000 to throw the World Series. Some of the players were more eager to participate in the deal than others, but they all agreed.

6   Chicago lost the first game, and then lost the second game as well, but the gamblers paid the players only a small fraction of what had been promised. The players' began to doubt the gamblers would uphold their part of the agreement, so they went out and played well in the next game and won. Many of the gamblers lost money and were unhappy about it, so they paid a bit more to keep the players on their side.

7   But the players were now divided; some of them refused to participate any further, while others decided the money was still worth it. The White Sox lost the next two games, but once again the gamblers failed to pay up. Now, all the players agreed: it had been a mistake to get involved with dishonest men. Each player would earn $5,000 for winning the World Series, so why not play hard and win? That's what they did, and Chicago won the next two games.

8   The series was now 4–3 in the Reds' favor. Cincinnati had to win only one more game to become World Series champions. To make sure that happened, one of the gamblers visited the home of the White Sox player who would pitch in the game. He threatened the pitcher and the pitcher's wife, and the result was that the frightened player caused Chicago to lose the next game. The Cincinnati Reds became the 1919 World Series champions.

9   No one discovered right away that the players had cheated. But gambling was affecting many other games, too, and officials began investigating cheating in baseball. A year after the White Sox players had thrown the World Series, the investigators finally looked into their games. The players faced a criminal trial. Some of them confessed about what had happened, but even so, they were all acquitted because of lack of evidence. However, all of the players were banned from playing professional baseball for the rest of their lives.

**I.** Which two teams played in the 1919 World Series?

_____ against _____

**2.** Why were the players unhappy?

_____

_____

**3.** Complete the following sentence.

If a player wanted to quit one team to go play for another team, first he had to

_____ .

**4.** What type of writing was this text? Place a checkmark on the line of the best answer.

_____ biography                    _____ historical nonfiction

_____ historical fiction           _____ persuasive essay

**5.** The author describes three main elements that led to the Black Sox Scandal. What are they?

_____

_____

_____

**6.** Do you think it was fair that the players involved in the scandal were banned from baseball for life? Why or why not?

_____

_____

_____

_____

**7.** Fables are fictional stories that often teach a lesson. They usually end with a moral, or a short statement that summarizes the lesson. What lesson do you think could be taught with this story? Write a moral to the story of the Black Sox Scandal.

_____

_____

_____

# Nice Hit!

*What happens when Victor comes up to bat?*

1   The two of them were whispering, but Victor could still hear what they were saying.

2   "But he's in a wheelchair!" the taller guy said. "How can he play?"

3   "I don't know," said the guy with dark hair, "but we're just practicing. If he says he can hit, why not? I'd like to see it."

4   Victor was used to the skepticism. Most people had no idea someone in a wheelchair could play baseball, but Victor had been playing wheelchair sports, including baseball, since he was young. The taller guy walked over to where Victor sat waiting.

5   "Sure, you can hit with us," he said. "My name's Zachary, and this is Matt." Zachary pointed in his friend's direction.

6   Victor introduced himself, and the three of them headed around the backstop and onto the field. Zachary jogged across the infield to the pitching mound, and Matt took his time strolling farther out, just past second base. Victor rolled his wheelchair up to home plate with the bat balanced skillfully across his thighs.

7   Victor greatly enjoyed all aspects of baseball—all aspects of all sports, really—but he particularly loved batting. That moment of anticipation as the pitcher casually looked around, apparently in no hurry to continue the game, stretching out the seconds, until finally winding up and sending the white blur hurtling across space. And then the power of the bat—the product of its weight multiplied by the motion—smacking hard against the ball and radically alternating its course, or better yet, reversing its course. Victor saw it all scientifically: physics and mathematics employed for fun and sport.

8   Now, Zachary was winding up; leg raised, arm back, *whoosh*! The ball accelerated out of Zachary's hand.

9   Victor's sharp eyes followed the white sphere as it zoomed straight toward him, and he knew right when—and where—to swing. The bat connected with the ball, and Victor sent it flying back toward the mound, a bit to the left. The ball landed between second base and third base, a half second ahead of Matt's glove. He had to chase it down as it skittered into the outfield.

10   "Nice!" yelled Zachary excitedly. "Fantastic hit, Victor!"

11   Zachary pitched several more times, and Victor got a hit on most of them. One sailed over Zachary's and Matt's heads and landed deep in center field. He could tell that both guys were impressed.

12   Zachary and Matt ran up to Victor, and they each gave him a high five. Matt was ready for a turn at bat, so he suggested that Victor head into the outfield. Victor pointed out that wheeling around on the turf would be difficult, so he stayed by the backstop and played catcher.

13   After each boy had his turn batting, they headed toward the bleachers. Zachary and Matt were curious to know how Victor had gotten so good at hitting.

14   "I've played on a wheelchair baseball team the last few years," Victor explained. He described how a wheelchair baseball diamond is different from a traditional baseball diamond. "The two are really similar, but the biggest difference is that for wheelchair baseball, the playing surface needs to be perfectly smooth.

15   "Another difference is that batters are allowed to use a kind of bracket for their wheelchairs when they bat. It's a metal frame lying on the ground that the wheelchair can attach to so it won't move. I've seen guys swing so hard at the ball, they tip their chairs right over!"

16   Victor glanced at his watch and saw it was time to head home for dinner. He invited Matt and Zachary to come see a wheelchair baseball game some time, and they both agreed that it would be a blast.

**1.** In your own words, describe the meaning of each word, based on how it is used in the story.

skepticism: _____

_____

particularly: _____

_____

product: _____

_____

**2.** What sentence best describes the theme of this story? Place a checkmark next to the best answer.

_____ Wheelchair baseball is no different than traditional baseball.

_____ A person in a wheelchair can be a great athlete.

_____ Batting is the best part of playing baseball.

_____ Baseball combines mathematics and physics for fun.

**3.** Why were Matt and Zachary impressed?

_____

_____

**4.** Why did Victor play catcher instead of heading to the outfield?

_____

_____

**5.** Why do batters in wheelchair baseball sometimes attach their wheelchairs to a metal frame?

_____

_____

**6.** In addition to what is explained in the story, describe two other ways that you think a wheelchair baseball game would differ from a traditional baseball game.

_____

_____

_____

# Building the Frozen Ark

*How can freezing cells help to save the world as we now know it?*

1     What do the mountain gorilla, the snow leopard, and the rosy tree snail have in common? Sadly, it is not something good. They are all endangered. You've probably heard the term *endangered* and even read about endangered animals. But what classifies an animal as endangered? What does that really mean? Endangered animals are animal species whose numbers are small and falling. The numbers are so small the species is at risk of extinction, or of dying out. As of January 2013, 2,054 species were considered endangered. Animal species extinction has many causes. One primary cause is habitat destruction caused by human population growth and pollution. Climate change, illegal trade, and over-fishing are other causes that can lead to a species' extinction.

2     What can be done to prevent extinction? Conservationists, people who work to protect our natural environment, work to preserve the species' environments. But even with these efforts, it is estimated that within 50 years, 30% of all land, marine, and fresh-water animals will be extinct. In 1996, another idea to save the animal species was born.

3     The Frozen Ark Project was developed to come to the aid of the endangered species. This project uses modern-day science technology to save species. Every living cell has DNA. DNA is the chemical substance of genes. DNA determines heredity in all living creatures. An interesting fact about DNA is that it is capable of making copies of itself.

4     Can you guess where the Frozen Ark Project got its name? The goal of the project is to freeze cell samples of the DNA of endangered animals. Just as with humans, a complete copy of DNA can be found in just one single cell. The developers of this project do not view this as a substitute to preserving the environment. Rather, they see it as an extra measure to save these animals.

5     You might be wondering if collecting these samples is harmful to the animals. The answer is *no*. Only very small samples are needed. Samples can be taken from hairs, feathers, mouth swabs, and even feces. The frozen cells can be stored safely for up to 100 years. Also, it does not take much room to store samples. It is suggested by current molecular biologists that it will soon be possible to regrow the frozen cells. These endangered species could then be revived.

6     The collection of DNA can help to preserve species once they are gone. It may also help the animals now. Knowing about an animal's DNA gives clues to its ecological needs. One example of this is a species' contact with environmental toxins. This information can be useful to veterinarians and conservation workers. Also, conservation biologists can ensure variety in animals' genetic makeup when regrowing cells. If animals that are already very close in DNA structure breed, problems often arise. Biologists can make sure the DNA is not so closely matched. This can lead to a healthier species. It can also lead to increased life expectancy.

7     The professionals involved in the project are very qualified. Biologists have research skills. They are also experts at sample collection and preservation. Conservationists are experts in animal species and environments. They also know how to collect samples in the wild. The Frozen Ark Project has many important members around the world. Supporters include zoos, museums, and aquariums.

8     All animal species will benefit from increased awareness and conservation efforts. And with support for projects such as Frozen Ark, our world may not have to lose the animal species that are such a vital part of our natural environment.

**1.** What is a *conservationist*? Use the text to help you write a definition.

_____

_____

**2.** Classify the following statements from the text by writing **O** if the statement is an opinion, or **F** if the statement is a fact.

_____ It is estimated that within 50 years, 30% of all land, marine, and fresh-water animals will be extinct.

_____ An interesting fact about DNA is that it is capable of making copies of itself.

_____ Knowing about an animal's DNA gives clues to its ecological needs.

_____ The frozen cells can be stored safely for up to 100 years.

_____ The professionals involved in the project are very qualified.

_____ Climate change, illegal trade, and over-fishing are other causes that can lead to a species' extinction.

**3.** What is the author's purpose for writing this text? Place a checkmark on the line of the best answer.

_____ to entertain          _____ to persuade

_____ to inform          _____ to explain

**4.** Is it harmful to the animals to collect DNA samples from them? Explain your answer.

_____

_____

**5.** Where does the Frozen Ark Project get its name? Place a checkmark on the line of the correct answer.

_____ The DNA samples are stored at a research facility located in Antarctica.

_____ The project is sponsored by Frozen Ark Foods, Inc.

_____ The project freezes animal cells to preserve their DNA.

_____ Scientists are concerned about mass extinctions that could result from a new ice age.

**6.** List three of the benefits provided by the Frozen Ark Projects.

_____

_____

_____

# Save the Manatees!

*When a new housing development threatens a local manatee habitat, what can Kayla do?*

1   At the bottom of the *Naple Island Gazette's* front page, Kayla saw the headline: *Manatee Habitat Threatened by Local Development.* The article explained that a new housing development was planned for an area along the Okee River. Many of the properties would have docks in the river so owners could park their boats and have easy access out into the bay. Kayla knew that the Okee River was the best place locally to spot manatees. They loved floating in the warm water and munching the thick sea grasses that covered the river bottom. Right now, it was the perfect habitat for manatees, but once motorboats started zooming up and down the river, it would no longer be perfect. In fact, it would be dangerous to them.

2   When Kayla arrived at school later that morning, she had the article—and a plan—ready to share with her classmates. She eagerly approached her teacher, Ms. Patel, and shared her ideas. Ms. Patel was impressed. She gave Kayla permission to address the class.

3   "Good morning, everyone!" Ms. Patel greeted her students. "Kayla has shared a bit of news with me this morning, and I'd like to give her a chance to let you know about it as well. Her plan will make a great project for us this semester."

4   Kayla began by describing what she knew about the housing development. Then, she continued with information about manatees.

5   "Manatees are sometimes called *sea cows.* Like cows, they're big, gentle mammals that love to eat grass. Of course, manatees live in the water and they graze on sea grass, and instead of hooves, they have flippers on the ends of their front legs, and instead of back legs, they have a giant flat tail. The reason they live along the coast and in the rivers around here is because they can't survive in water that is too deep or too cold. Warm, shallow water is the perfect habitat for them. They can easily float to the surface and breathe, and then they can float back down to the bottom, where they chow on sea grasses.

6   "This development will wreck one of the best manatee habitats around here. The biggest problem will be the boats. Manatees are really slow. They can't get out of the way when a speedboat comes racing along. The spinning propeller blades can slice up a manatee's back enough to kill it. It's common for manatees to have scars all over their backs from encounters with boats."

7   Kayla explained other problems that people can cause, such as feeding the manatees food that is not good for them, scaring the manatees away from protective habitats, or even injuring manatees by trying to ride them or otherwise abusing them.

8   "My plan has two parts," Kayla continued. "We'll start with a fundraiser. I looked online and found a local group called the *Manatee Protection Service.* They already work hard to preserve manatee habitats, so helping them will be the best first step. They can use all the money they can get, so we'll donate to them whatever we earn.

9   "The second part of my plan is to meet with the developer," Kayla explained. "Speedboats are the most immediate threat to manatees' lives, and the slower a boat goes, the less chance it has of injuring a manatee. I think we can work with the developer to set up a slow speed limit along the river. That's happened in other places, so I think we have a good chance of making that work here too."

10   Kayla was finished, and she could tell her classmates were excited. A buzz filled the room as everyone started speaking at once. Ideas for the fundraiser were flying—a car wash, a bake sale, an art auction, a raffle—and Kayla smiled as she thought, *I guess human activities aren't always bad for the manatees.*

**1.** How does Kayla learn about the threat to the manatees' habitat?

_____

**2.** What are the two parts of Kayla's plan?

_____

_____

_____

**3.** List three characteristics of manatees described in the story.

_____

_____

_____

**4.** Why is the setting important in this story?

_____

_____

_____

**5.** What does Kayla mean by the statement, *I guess human activities aren't <u>always</u> bad for the manatees*?

_____

_____

_____

**6.** Do you think Kayla's plan will work? Why or why not?

_____

_____

_____

_____

**7.** What animals are common where you live? Describe how human activities might affect the habitats of these animals.

_____

_____

_____

# Slow—Manatee Xing

*What would you do if you discovered an injured animal?*

1    Tyler Jones looked back toward the horizon, the sun blazing high overhead. He felt exhausted, but in a satisfying way. He and his father had spent the morning out on the boat, bobbing with the ocean waves as they tried for hours to catch the perfect fish. Tyler had caught a few flounder, but the prize of the day was a ten-pound kingfish hauled in by Mr. Jones. He was radioing home to Tyler's mother to suggest that she invite the neighbors over for dinner: ten pounds was a lot of fish!

2    As they approached the mouth of the Longtooth River—Tyler's family lived about ten minutes upstream—Mr. Jones slowed the boat down. They chugged along at about jogging speed, when suddenly a speedboat came flying up the river in the opposite direction, headed out to sea. It roared past them, going much too fast, and Mr. Jones shook his head.

3    "Some folks just have no sense," he sighed.

4    They turned from the open water and headed upstream, Longtooth River opening up wide in front of them. This part of the river was still wild and undeveloped, with grassy inlets and marshlands lining both sides. Tyler always enjoyed this stretch because he often spotted manatees floating near the shore, their broad, gray-brown backs breaking the surface. Sometimes he would even catch site of a whiskery snout poking from the water for a breath of air.

5    Tyler's eyes were scanning the water for manatees when he saw it: a large smear of red drifting up ahead of the boat. He pointed and asked, "Is that what I think it is?"

6    "Yeah, that's blood," confirmed Mr. Jones. When they got closer, they looked down through the cloudy water and saw a manatee floating just below the surface, a gaping wound open across its back. "That boat that sped through here? I'm pretty sure it zipped right across this poor guy's back and cut him right up."

7    Mr. Jones quickly radioed the Wildlife Rescue Patrol and explained what they had discovered. A voice on the other end asked if they could stick around for a couple of hours until rescuers got there. Mr. Jones radioed his wife to let her know they would be late.

8    Three hours later, the rescuers arrived in two surprisingly small boats. One of the boats was open at the back. About ten men and women made up the Wildlife Rescue Patrol. One man briefly thanked Tyler and Mr. Jones, and then they all went to work.

9    Several of the rescuers dove into the water with large sections of netting. Tyler found it difficult to follow exactly what was happening, because half the time they were underwater, but eventually they had the injured manatee wrapped in the netting.

10    Next, the rescuers dragged the netting, along with the manatee, toward the boat with the open back. Tyler soon understood why the boat was designed like it was: the rescuers could drag the manatee straight onto the boat without having to lift the animal up and over the side. Still, the manatee weighed several hundred pounds, and it took all of the rescuers pushing and pulling together to get the job done.

11    As the boat with the manatee headed off, one of the rescuers who remained explained that it was being taken to a rehabilitation facility, where the injury would be treated and it would have a safe place to recover. If everything went well, the manatee would be released back into the wild after it had completely healed.

12    The rescuers in the second boat thanked Mr. Jones and Tyler for calling them, and then just like that, they were gone, too. The river seemed strangely quiet.

13    "Well, I guess it's our turn to head home," said Mr. Jones. He fired up the boat, and they moved slowly—and carefully—up the river and toward a well-deserved fish dinner.

**1.** Which point of view is used in telling this story: first-person, second-person, or third-person? Explain how you know.

_____

_____

**2.** Identify the order of events in the story by writing 1–8 on the lines.

_____ The rescuers wrapped the injured manatee in a net.

_____ Mr. Jones radioed the Wildlife Rescue Patrol.

_____ Mr. Jones caught a kingfish.

_____ Tyler and Mr. Jones saw the injured manatee.

_____ The rescuers dragged the manatee onto the boat.

_____ Mr. Jones radioed his wife to say he and Tyler would be late.

_____ Tyler saw blood in the water.

_____ The speedboat raced past Tyler and Mr. Jones.

**3.** The author wrote "the speedboat came flying up the river . . . " Explain why this is an example of figurative language, rather than a literal, or actual, description of what happened.

_____

_____

**4.** As Mr. Jones approaches the mouth of the Longtooth River, he slows down. Why do you think he does this?

_____

_____

**5.** The author never explicitly states what time of day the story takes place, so how do you know? Cite evidence from the text to support your answer.

_____

_____

**6.** What do Mr. Jones's and Tyler's actions tell you about them? Cite evidence from the text to support your answer.

_____

_____

# The Festival of Lights

*What traditions mark the Hindu festival of Diwali?*

1   Dev hurried home from school to get ready for the party. Today was the third day of Diwali—the Hindu "festival of lights"—and this year, the main festivities were being held at his family's home. All of his relatives would be arriving in about an hour, and he wanted to help out with any preparations that were left to do. Dev's mother, Mrs. Mehta, along with his grandmother, aunts, and sisters, had been cooking all sorts of *mithai*—little sweet and savory snacks—for the last couple of weeks. Trays of mithai would be set around the house for guests to munch on as they celebrated the last day of the year.

2   In front of the Mehta's home, clay pots with sparklers lined the front porch. The clay lamps would be lit around dusk in order to attract Lakshmi to their home. She is the goddess of wealth, and her presence would bring good luck to their family for the coming year. The lights also symbolized positivity by keeping out the darkness. Dev remembered a Diwali festival he had attended once that ended with a huge fireworks display, bright colors exploding across the night sky. Lakshmi certainly didn't miss those lights!

3   Dev bounded through the front door and called out to his mother, "Hi! I'm home!" Mrs. Mehta was hard at work in the kitchen preparing the main dishes for the party. She was cooking vegetable biryani, cardamom chicken curry, and Dev's favorite: sag paneer. He loved the creamy spinach sag mixed with jasmine rice, but it was the chewy paneer, or chunks of cheese, hiding in the sauce that he loved most.

4   "We're very close to being ready," Dev's mother explained, "so why don't you head upstairs and get dressed."

5   Up in his room, Dev changed into a traditional Indian outfit: a pair of silk pants with a matching kurta on top. The kurta was a long, loose shirt that came to his knees. It did not have a collar. Dev wore a kurta only a few times a year, so it was always a special occasion when he did.

6   Dev went back downstairs, and his mother asked him to do a few last minute chores. He took out the garbage, he straightened the pillows in the living room, and he lit all the candles and incense placed around the house.

7   In the living room, Dev admired the rangoli displayed on the floor. The rug had been rolled back, and in the middle of the room was a large, intricate design made of colorful powders. Dev and his sister, Avani, had designed the circular pattern for the rangoli, and then the rest of the family had helped carefully pour the powders. He was always a little sad when Diwali was over, and the powders had to be swept up.

8   The doorbell rang, and it was Aunt Nita, Uncle Darsh, and Dev's cousin Aarav. Uncle Darsh and Aarav were both dressed in kurtas. Aunt Nita wore a festive sari. The sari was a very long piece of cloth wrapped around her waist to form a kind of skirt. The rest of the long cloth was wrapped around her upper body and draped over her shoulder. Dev's mother, dressed in a sari as well, came from the kitchen to welcome them and admire her sister's outfit.

9   All at once, the other relatives began to arrive. Dev could hear poor Chico, his dog, barking from the room upstairs where he was locked up. Chico wanted to be part of the Diwali celebration, too, but last year he had trampled right through the rangoli and spread colored powder all over the house. So Dev and Aarav grabbed a couple of platefuls of *mithai* and raced up to see Chico. They had plenty of snacks for themselves—and for Chico, too!

**I.** In your own words, explain why Diwali is called "The Festival of Lights."

_____

_____

_____

**2.** Who is Lakshmi? Place a checkmark on the line of the best answer.

_____ the goddess of wealth          _____ the goddess of light

_____ the goddess of the new year          _____ the goddess of positivity

**3.** Use context clues to define each of the following terms from the text:

sari: _____

sag paneer: _____

mithai: _____

rangoli: _____

kurta: _____

**4.** What nation did Dev's ancestors most likely come from? Place a checkmark on the line of the best answer.

_____ Egypt          _____ England

_____ India          _____ Japan

**5.** Choose an adjective that you think describes Dev. Support your choice with evidence from the story.

_____

_____

_____

_____

**6.** What cultural holiday or tradition is most important to you? Describe what it is and why it is important to you.

_____

_____

_____

_____

# Mohandas Gandhi

*How did a shy, average student become one of history's most admired people?*

1    "An eye for an eye only ends up making the whole world blind." These wise words were spoken by one of the 20th century's most important leaders. This man never ruled a country as president or prime minister, and he never led military troops or owned a multimillion-dollar company. What he did was perhaps even more astounding. He led millions of people in nonviolent protests that ended with one of history's most powerful empires withdrawing from his beloved country.

2    Mohandas Gandhi was born on October 2, 1869, in Porbandar, India. When he was young, he was shy and an average student. However, he was also lucky to be born into India's merchant caste. In India, society is divided into different social castes, or groups. Those who belong to higher castes usually have more wealth. They are more respected, and they have access to a better education. So while Gandhi was attending college in India, he was offered the chance to study law in London, England. He jumped at the chance and headed four thousand miles west.

3    Soon after Gandhi earned his law degree, he found work in South Africa. He spent the next 21 years living there. At the time, racial segregation was a fact of life in South Africa. As an Indian, Gandhi experienced the daily struggle of living in an unfair and prejudiced system. He became determined to fight back, but his religious and spiritual beliefs led him to reject violent methods. Instead, he strongly believed that nonviolence could be used to make great changes.

4    Over time, Gandhi developed the idea of *satyagraha,* which means *truth force.* It was a form of protesting injustice without using violence or anger. Gandhi believed that this approach would result in a peaceful solution to a conflict. This idea was put to the test when Gandhi and others protested laws in South Africa requiring Indians to carry identification at all time. The law treated Indians unequally. The process of *satyagraha* was not easy or quick, and the protesters were often beaten and imprisoned. But after seven long years, the protestors won, and the laws were changed.

5    When Gandhi returned home to India in 1915, he was famous because of his role in changing the laws of South Africa. He was honored with the title "Mahatma," which means "Great Soul." But Gandhi was not fond of the title; he considered himself simply one of the people. To reinforce this idea, Gandhi began wearing the simple clothing of the poor. It was how he would dress for the rest of his life.

6    During this time, India was ruled by the British Empire, and in 1930, Gandhi led perhaps his most famous protest: the march against the British salt tax. British law stated that it was illegal for Indians to buy salt that was not sold by the government. Gandhi marched more than 200 miles to the sea to collect his own salt. Along the way, more and more Indians joined the protest. By the time Gandhi reached the sea, there were more than 2,000 people with him. Indians began making or collecting their own salt. Those who protested against the salt tax were repeatedly attacked and beaten, but they did not fight back. In the end, Britain's rulers understood that attacking peaceful protesters made the Empire appear brutal, violent, and uncivilized.

7    The salt march was just one step in the long journey toward Indian independence. Gandhi continued using peaceful means to work for the goal of ending British rule. He was imprisoned many times for his nonviolent actions. In 1947, India finally achieved independence from British rule.

8    Sadly, Gandhi's life was cut short the next year. In January of 1948, an assassin shot him as he headed to a prayer meeting in Delhi. Despite the violence that ended his life, the powerful results of Gandhi's nonviolent life inspired others, including Nelson Mandela and Martin Luther King, Jr.

**I.** Which of the genres listed below best describes the text? Place a checkmark on the line of the best choice.

_____ biography                    _____ historical nonfiction

_____ autobiography              _____ historical fiction

**2.** Classify the following statements as **T** if a statement is true or **F** if a statement is false.

_____ "Mahatma" is an honorable title meaning *truth force*.

_____ Gandhi was born in India, attended college in England, and lived much of his life in South Africa.

_____ Gandhi wore simple clothes because he was born into a lower caste.

_____ The powerful salt march protest marked the end of British rule in India.

**3.** The author describes Gandhi as one of the 20th century's most important leaders. What evidence does the author cite to support this idea?

_____

_____

_____

_____

**4.** Why did Gandhi dislike the title "Mahatma"?

_____

_____

**5.** Based on what you've read about Gandhi, choose three words to describe him. Explain why you chose each word.

I. _____

_____

2. _____

_____

3. _____

_____

# Life in the Mangrove Forest

*Have you heard of the forest that is home to hundreds of species of life—from birds, to fish, to pythons, to big cats? It's a far away place that is closer than you may think.*

1    Have you ever heard of the trees that are homes to animals both on land and sea? These beautiful and complex trees are called *mangroves*. The forests of mangroves are an important part of life on this planet.

2    Mangrove trees, it is believed, originated in Southeast Asia. That is where most of the forests can still be found today. They are, however, found throughout Earth, but mostly within 30 degrees of the equator. They cannot tolerate freezing temperatures. They grow mostly in slow-moving waters. An identifier of a mangrove tree is its dense formation of roots. This root system enables the trees to hold their own with the coming and going of daily tides. Coastline mangrove forests act as guards from the sea to the land. They reduce erosion from waves and tides. They protect sea creatures from predators in their elaborate root infrastructure. Birds and fish can both call a mangrove home.

3    The world's largest mangrove forest is called the *Sundarban Reserve Forest*. The Sundarbans is located southwest of Bangladesh on the Bay of Bengal. It is between the Baleswar River and the Harinbanga River. Most of the forest lies in Bangladesh and the remaining part in India.

4    In addition to hundreds of species of birds and plants, the Sundarbans is home to many endangered species. The Bengal tiger, Ganges and Irawadi dolphins, the river terrapin (river turtle), the estuarine crocodile, and the Indian python all reside in the Sundarbans. In fact, one species, the Panthera tigris, is now only found in the Sundarbans. The Panthera tigris (of which the Bengal tiger is a subspecies) is the world's largest cat.

5    It is estimated that the Sundarbans has a habitat of 334 plant and 693 wildlife species. The wildlife species is broken down into 49 mammals, 59 reptiles, 8 amphibians, 210 white fish, 24 shrimp, 14 crab, and 43 mollusks species. Three hundred and fifteen species of waterfowl, raptors, and forest birds inhabit the Sundarbans.

6    Unfortunately, threats do exist to this ecologically rich environment. The threats are both natural and human. Cyclones and tidal waves have taken a toll on the forest trees and some of its species. Humans illegally hunt, farm, and collect timber from the forest.

7    To help protect against human threats, three wildlife sanctuaries were established in the forest in 1977. The Bangladesh Wildlife Preservation Act attempts to control illegal entry, fishing, and hunting in the forest. Other groups from around the world have become involved with the preservation of the Sundarbans and its inhabitants. The World Wildlife Fund, the National Zoological Park, and the Smithsonian Institution are working on conservation and wildlife management programs.

8    Protection of this environment is important not only to the endangered animal species, but also to the humans who live near it. The Sundarbans provide a safety zone against cyclones, tidal waves, and other storms. The Sundarbans also provide some local jobs.

9    While the Sundarbans and its inhabitants seem like they exist in a remote part of our world, they really are closer than you may think. The Sundarbans, in some respect, belong to us all. The Sundarbans is a UNESCO World Heritage Site. UNESCO stands for United Nations Educational, Scientific, and Cultural Organization. UNESCO seeks to identify World Heritage Sites to protect and preserve cultural and natural heritages of the world. The sites are considered to be of outstanding value to humanity. According to the organization, World Heritage Sites belong to all people, regardless of where they are located. This beautiful forest and all of its creatures depend on all of us to protect and preserve, just as we depend on them.

**I.** What is the main idea of the passage? Place a checkmark next to the sentence that most closely describes them main idea of the passage.

_____ Humans illegally hunt, farm, and collect timber from the Sundarbans.

_____ The Sundarban Reserve Forest is the largest mangrove forest on Earth.

_____ The Sundarban Reserve Forest is a unique and important environmental site that needs to be protected.

_____ Mangrove forests support an amazingly diverse number of plants and animals, and they help reduce erosion of the coastline.

**2.** On the lines below, write three facts about mangrove forests.

1. _____

2. _____

3. _____

**3.** What does UNESCO stand for?

_____

**4.** Describe the author's viewpoint about mangrove forests. Use evidence from the text to support your answer.

_____

_____

**5.** Write three sentences summarizing the second paragraph.

1. _____

2. _____

3. _____

**6.** Describe a natural environment that is important or special to you, such as a park, nature preserve, or other outdoor place. What makes it a special place?

_____

_____

**7.** If you learned that this special place was threatened by development, what do you think you could to help protect it?

_____

_____

# A Monument to Love

*What is the story behind the Taj Mahal, recognized as one of the most beautiful buildings in the world?*

1   Prince Khurram strolled quietly through the crowded marketplace, eyeing the rich array of fruits, vegetables, meats, and crafts displayed in stall after stall. The faces of the four palace guards keeping pace with the 14-year-old prince held stern expressions. In contrast, Prince Khurram grinned broadly. He enjoyed being out among the common people as they went about their normal daily chores, and the idea pleased him greatly that one day he would become their emperor. This was not because he craved power, but because he was proud of the Indian people. He wished nothing less than to lead them to even greater successes.

2   The prince's father was the current emperor, and his grandfather was Akbar the Great, the most revered emperor yet of the Mughal Empire. Prince Khurram was Akbar's favorite among his many grandsons, and this assured his rise to the throne.

3   As the prince's gaze wandered the many sights of the market, it fell upon a lovely young woman examining colorful strings of beads in a jeweler's stall. Prince Khurram stopped breathing and stared with such intensity that the guards became worried. They inquired about his condition, and the prince explained with a single, short phrase: "I'm in love."

4   It was apparent from her fine clothing and graceful manner that she was most likely born of nobility, but Prince Khurram had never seen her before. He quickly dispatched one of his guards to learn her name and convey this message: "With a single glance, you have entered my heart. I know as certain as the sun rises each day, I will love you forever."

5   Her name was Arjumand Banu Begum, and she was indeed the daughter of noble parents. Arjumand was flattered by the prince's words, and she agreed to meet him and see if she felt the same. As soon as Prince Khurram left the market, he traveled to the home of Arjumand's parents and met with her father. The prince declared his love and his intentions to marry her. Arjumand's father consented to the prince's wish to meet her and get to know her, but as for marriage, that would need to wait.

6   And so it was five years later that Prince Khurran and Arjumand Banu Begum were married in a lavish, royal ceremony. The years went by, and they had many children. Their love for one another grew stronger by the day. Then, as the prince had predicted many years before, he became Shah Jahan, emperor of the Mughal Empire. His beloved bride was renamed Mumtaz Mahal, meaning "the jewel of the palace."

7   As emperor, Shah Jahan often traveled to distant lands within the empire, and Mumtaz accompanied him wherever he went. Their deep love and constant companionship were admired by the Indian people. Poets throughout the land celebrated their relationship. But then, after nearly 20 years of marriage, tragedy struck.

8   Mumtaz Mahal died during the delivery of their fourteenth child. Shah Jahan was inconsolable. For one year he mourned, secluded inside his palace and refusing all visitors. When he reemerged at last, the emperor looked much older: his hair had turned white, he stooped at the waist, and deep wrinkles lined his face. But Shah Jahan had a plan that would honor his late wife in a manner grand enough to reflect the enormity of their love.

9   In the city of Agra, along the banks of the River Yamuna, a massive project was begun. Thousands of laborers worked for more than 20 years to construct the largest and most beautiful mausoleum in all of history. The giant, white marble tomb was topped by a magnificent dome. A towering minaret stood at each of the four corners. Lush gardens and glassy pools adorned the surrounding landscape. The symmetrical perfection of the building and grounds announced to the world that theirs had been a perfect love. And the Taj Mahal still stands today as the world's greatest monument to love.

**I.** The Taj Mahal is a real place, and Shah Jahan and Mumtaz Mahal were real people. Which of the following genres of writing best describes the text? Place a checkmark on the line of the best answer.

_____ fable                    _____ historical nonfiction

_____ folk tale                _____ biography

As indicated, provide either a cause or an effect to complete each cause-and-effect relationship below. There may be more than one possible answer, but the cause or effect you provide must make sense according to events in story.

**2. cause:** Prince Khurran sees Arjumand Banu Begum at the market.

   **effect:** _____

**3. cause:** _____

   **effect:** Arjumand Banu Begum is renamed Mumtaz Mahal.

**4. cause:** _____

   **effect:** Shah Jahan orders the construction of the Taj Mahal.

**5.** Provide your own example of a cause-and-effect relationship from the story.

   **cause:** _____

   **effect:** _____

**6.** Reread the story. Draw a conclusion about which elements were most likely invented by the author, and which are mostly likely historical facts. List three of each below.

   Fact: _____

   Fact: _____

   Fact: _____

   Fiction: _____

   Fiction: _____

   Fiction: _____

**7.** Explain how you determined which parts were fact and which were fiction.

   _____

   _____

   _____

   _____

# The Imperfect Gift of Memory

*What if you could remember everything?*

1   Imagine you could remember everything that ever happened to you. The details of every book you have ever read, clear in your mind as the moment your eyes first took in each sentence. Every moment in class etched flawlessly into your memory, so all the information is at your fingertips when you take a test or a quiz. The route to any place you've ever been, even if it was just one time many years ago, mapped in your mind so you can return without needing directions. A perfect memory sounds like a wish come true, doesn't it?

2   But as the old saying goes, *Be careful what you wish for.* Believe it or not, there are a select number of people in the world who have near perfect memories of their experiences. They remember almost every detail about almost every day of their lives. People with this ability are designated as having a "highly superior autobiographical memory," or HSAM. Scientists estimate that less than 100 people in the United States have HSAM, and many of them would argue that this apparent gift is really a curse.

3   If you were asked this evening to describe the events of your day in as much detail as possible, you would probably do pretty well. You would recall what you ate for breakfast, who you spoke with during English class, the main subject discussed in social studies, and what you did before dinner. But what if I asked you to provide details about what you did on March 3, 2012. Do you know what day of the week it was? What did you eat for lunch? Was it cold that day? Sunny? Chances are you would have no idea where to even begin.

4   A person with HSAM would be able to provide all those details and more for almost any day of his or her life, regardless of how many years in the past the day occurred. Even if that sounds like a neat trick, it certainly has its drawbacks. In addition to every great moment they remember, they also remember—in great detail—each time they were embarrassed or deeply sad. They remember every moment someone made them angry. They remember every mistake they ever made. Those with HSAM often suffer from depression. The negative events replay in their minds in equal detail as the great moments. Sometimes, forgetting isn't such a bad thing.

5   In fact, for most of us, forgetting is a natural part of how our brains function. If we don't need to remember something or try to make an effort to remember it, the information fades away and is lost. But for those people with HSAM, it is not so much that they have excellent memories; it is that they are unable to forget. All of their experiences, even the most mundane or unimportant, remain accessible to them all the time.

6   Research has shown that the brains of people with HSAM do not simply function differently than other brains; their brains are structurally different. They contain more connections in the white matter. White matter in the brain is associated with learning and how the brain functions. Gray matter is associated with thinking and processing information.

7   Scientists are working to determine how the difference in white matter affects those with HSAM. They also want to know *why* people with HSAM have different brains. Were they born with this difference, or did the difference develop during childhood? Research has shown that the brains of children with more than a year of musical training will exhibit structural changes. Perhaps adults with HSAM somehow trained their brains at an early age to remember their experiences and, over time, this training led to structural changes.

8   By studying the brains of people with HSAM, scientists may be able to find ways of helping others have better memories—not *perfect* memories with an inability to forget, but *better* memories.

**1.** What does *HSAM* stand for? Place a checkmark on the line of the correct answer.

_____ highly selective automatic memory

_____ highly superior autobiographical memory

_____ highly specialized aptitude for memorization

_____ highly selective analysis of memorization

**2.** Based on information in the text, which of the following conclusions could you draw? Place a checkmark on the line of the best answer.

_____ People with HSAM often work in fields such as astrophysics, neuroscience, or theoretical mathematics.

_____ People with HSAM have an unusual ability to remember events and experiences from their lives, but they are not necessarily more intelligent than all other people.

_____ People with HSAM have an unusual ability to remember events and experiences from their lives, but they have difficulty remembering facts that are unrelated to their personal experiences.

_____ People with HSAM have more negative experiences in their lives, often due to their unique ability to remember so much.

**3.** Why does the author write, *Sometimes forgetting isn't such a bad thing*?

_____

_____

**4.** In your own words, explain the difference between white matter and gray matter in the brain.

_____

_____

_____

**5.** The author states that some researchers wonder if HSAM is the result of physical changes in the brain that occur in childhood. What evidence is provided to show that this idea is a possibility?

_____

_____

**6.** Imagine you have HSAM. Describe one positive result of having HSAM. Then, describe one negative result.

_____

# Helping with Alzheimers

*How might you assist an older adult with Alzheimer's disease?*

1  Riding her bicycle home from school, Esperanza turns the corner and notices Mrs. Pellegrino standing in the middle of the sidewalk, holding her beloved cat, Charlotte. Esperanza parks her bike and smiles as she walks up to greet Mrs. Pellegrino.

2  "Hi, Mrs. Pellegrino," says Esperanza. "Where are you going?"

3  Mrs. Pellegrino doesn't return Esperanza's smile or answer the question, but instead she looks a little bit confused. Esperanza remembers her parents telling her that Mrs. Pellegrino has Alzheimer's disease, which causes people to become confused and have trouble remembering. Mrs. Pellegrino appears somewhat dazed right now, so Esperanza decides to help.

4  "It looks like we might have a thunderstorm soon," she declares. "Why don't I help you get Charlotte home?"

5  Esperanza extends her hand to Mrs. Pellegrino, who gratefully accepts it, and the pair begin walking down Russet Street toward Mrs. Pellegrino's condominium a block away. As they ascend the stairway, Mrs. Pellegrino begins to smile. "I couldn't remember the way home, and I was beginning to worry," she says. Esperanza returns her smile, escorting Mrs. Pellegrino and Charlotte indoors. Satisfied that they are now secure, Esperanza retrieves her bicycle and rides home. Pedaling into the garage, she is relieved to see that her mother's car is there. Esperanza wants to discuss what just happened.

6  "Mom," she says, walking into the kitchen, "I just helped Mrs. Pellegrino find her way home. She was on the next block, but she didn't seem to remember where she lived. She must have been following Charlotte and got confused."

7  Esperanza's mom looks at her with furrowed eyebrows and then walks over to the desk where she keeps her book with important phone numbers.

8  "I have her daughter's number here. Why don't we telephone her and make sure she knows what happened. I'm certain she'll want to hear about this, because if Mrs. Pellegrino's Alzheimer's is getting worse, she could accidentally injure herself. After we call, let's go over and talk to her for a bit."

9  Esperanza and her mom call Mrs. Pellegrino's daughter, who thanks them for letting her know about the situation and says she will be at her mother's house in a few minutes. As they head over to Mrs. Pellegrino's condominium, Esperanza's mom tells her a little more about Alzheimer's disease. Esperanza discovers that confusion and memory loss are the symptoms most people know about, but other symptoms of Alzheimer's include difficulty understanding visual images, losing the ability to retrace steps, withdrawal from social activities, and changes in mood and personality. Esperanza resolves to help Mrs. Pellegrino as much as she can. She often has a few hours free after school, and she resolves to spend some of that time with Mrs. Pellegrino. She could help run errands or complete other tasks that might be challenging because of the Alzheimer's disease.

10  "I'm proud of you, Esperanza," says her mom. " I know that Mrs. Pellegrino's daughter has a part-time job and children as well, so she'll probably be happy for your help. Let's go see what we can do to make Mrs. Pellegrino's experience with Alzheimer's disease more bearable."

11  Esperanza smiles and squeezes her mom's hand as they walk down the street to help their neighbor.

**1.** Is this story fiction or nonfiction? How do you know?

_____

_____

**2.** What is the author's main purpose? Support your answer with evidence from the text.

_____

_____

_____

_____

**3.** What details does the author include to show that Mrs. Pellegrino has Alzheimer's disease?

_____

_____

_____

**4.** Which of the following is NOT included in the text as a symptom of Alzheimer's disease? Place a checkmark on the line of the correct answer.

_____ memory loss                          _____ more likely to be injured

_____ changes in personality               _____ withdrawal from social activities

**5.** Who is Charlotte? Place a checkmark on the line of the correct answer.

_____ Esperanza's mom                      _____ Mrs. Pellegrino's daughter

_____ Mrs. Pellegrino's cat                _____ Mrs. Pellegrino's first name

**6.** How will Esperanza help Mrs. Pellegrino?

_____

**7.** What does the story tell you about Esperanza?

_____

_____

**8.** Why is it important to help our neighbors? Describe something you have done or plan to do to help one of your neighbors.

_____

_____

# Give Your Brain a Workout

*What steps can you take to improve your memory?*

Whether you need to memorize the dates of battles from the Civil War, or you're trying to remember the names of all the players on your favorite football team, having a good memory is key. Follow these tips to increase your brain power, and you will experience the benefits throughout your life.

- **Use your brain.** That may sound simplistic, but you need to use it or lose it. Similar to the way muscles in your body get stronger with physical exercise, you can strengthen your brain through mental exercise. Crossword puzzles, Sudoku, and other thinking games help keep your brain sharp. Scientists believe these mental workouts help activate synaptic connections in the brain. Synaptic connections are where the cells in your brain communicate with one another; the more connections there are, the better the brain functions.

- **Get enough sleep.** You may imagine your brain shutting down for the night, but in fact, your brain is active all night long. While you sleep, your brain processes and organizes all the events and information from your day. A good night's sleep will help you recall what you learned during the day. A seventh-grader should get a solid eight hours of sleep each night.

- **Eat brain food.** All the cells in your body need nutritious foods to grow and remain healthy, but certain foods are particularly good for brain cells. Much of the brain consists of healthy fat cells, and one of the most important is Omega-3 fatty acid. Foods that are high in Omega-3s are salmon, albacore tuna, walnuts, and eggs. Antioxidants are also good for your brain, because they eliminate substances called free radicals that can damage brain cells. Good sources of antioxidants include blueberries, broccoli, carrots, spinach, and tomatoes.

- **Focus.** If you can't remember where you put your math homework, maybe it's because, when you set it down, you were also listening to the TV while texting a friend as your mother asked you to set the table. In order to remember something, it has to get into your brain in the first place. People who tend to multi-task often miss information because they are not paying full attention. When they can't recall the information later on, they wonder why they can't remember it. Slow down and focus on the task at hand.

- **Use memory tools.** Memory tools are also called *mnemonic devices*. They are techniques to help you remember specific facts or information. You can create acronyms using the first letters of the information. For example, the name *ROY G. BIV* describes the main colors of the spectrum: red, orange, yellow, green, blue, indigo, violet. Initial letters can also be used for different words in order to form an easy-to-remember sentence. *My Very Excited Mother Just Served Us Noodles* describes the planets of our solar system: Mercury, Venus, Earth, Mars, Jupiter, Saturn, Uranus, Neptune.

- **Relax.** Being stressed has negative affects on memory. Your mind focuses on whatever is causing the stress, rather than focusing on whatever you need to remember. Researchers have even shown that the hippocampus—a part of the brain responsible for some memories—can shrink due to chronic, or continuous, stress.

**1.** Which of the following is NOT a suggestion from the text for improving your memory?

_____ Eat the right foods.          _____ Take memory enhancing pills.

_____ Get enough sleep.            _____ Use memory tools.

**2.** Write a sentence summarizing the main idea of the text.

_____

_____

**3.** Why does the author say relaxing can help improve your memory?

_____

_____

**4.** The paragraphs in the text are organized as a bulleted list. Why do you think the author chose to organize the text this way? Do you think this was or was not a good way to organize the information? Explain your answer.

_____

_____

_____

_____

_____

_____

**5.** Create a sentence to use as a mnemonic device for remembering the names of the original Thirteen Colonies: Delaware, Pennsylvania, New Jersey, Georgia, Connecticut, Massachusetts, Maryland, South Carolina, North Carolina, New Hampshire, Virginia, New York, Rhode Island.

_____

_____

_____

**6.** Which two suggestions from the text would be easiest for you to put into practice first? Explain why.

_____

_____

_____

# Catching up with the Past

*What might you learn by talking to others about life in the previous century?*

**Characters:** Frederick, a seventh-grade boy
Grandpa Davidson, an 85-year-old man

**Setting:** A plain kitchen with a table and two chairs; a window looks out onto a garden where two women are digging

*Frederick enters the kitchen and is pleased to discover that his Grandfather Davidson has come for a visit.*

**Frederick:** Grandpa Davidson! I am thrilled to see you! We have a school assignment that I'd love your help with. We are supposed to interview someone we respect about his or her childhood. Can I ask you some personal questions?

**Grandpa Davidson** (*chuckling*): You want to interview me?

*Frederick nods and extracts a notebook and ballpoint pen from his backpack.*

**Frederick:** We drafted questions in class today, so if you don't object, I'll just start asking them. I wanted to interview you for this assignment all along, so I'm delighted that you're here. First, I'd like to learn about your earliest memory.

**Grandpa Davidson:** Well, that'll take some thought. (*pauses*) Okay, as an infant I lived in the city of Philadelphia, but when I was six we moved to the country because my brother had asthma and the doctors thought that the fresh air would be better for him. Winter was my favorite season, because whenever a snowstorm came, we were allowed to remain home. So my earliest memory is riding my sled. We lived on an avenue that steeply sloped, and there was little vehicle traffic in the winter, so we navigated our sleds directly down the middle of the avenue. That's my earliest memory, probably because it was incredibly enjoyable.

**Frederick:** So you moved to a farm outside of Philadelphia. What animals did you have?

**Grandpa Davidson:** Dad worked in the poultry industry, so we definitely had chickens, and your Great-Great-Grandmother Davidson cooked many of them for our dinners. We actually sold eggs at the end of our driveway for 10 cents a dozen, and once a month we would sell them at a market in Philadelphia. We had horses, cows, sheep, and barn cats. We had a giant dog named Spartacus that we loved. I always enjoyed sledding, and Spartacus was so tremendously large that sometimes we hitched a sled to him! It wasn't cruel—that dog was so massive that he hardly realized we were attached behind him, and we often capsized because Spartacus would begin running and turn so sharply that he tipped over the sled.

**Frederick** (*laughing*): That's a funny story, Grandpa! I can almost picture it. So what chores were you assigned on the farm?

**Grandpa Davidson:** Our entire family worked hard, but one of my biggest jobs was helping with plowing. We planted and harvested corn and buckwheat. In the beginning, we didn't own a gasoline-powered tractor, so we hitched the horses to a plow, and let me tell you, that plow was difficult to navigate. By the end of every day our muscles ached from holding those horses steady. Another responsibility was looking after the animals' health. We arose early each day to tend our livestock, and worked long into the night as well.

**Frederick:** What is one enjoyable thing you did?

**Grandpa Davidson:** The animals were a lot of work, but one of the great benefits of having them came during the annual state fair. Our family would display our animals at competitions, and I still have a collection of blue ribbons to remember those days by. Remind me to show you those ribbons when you visit next time. They're important to me because they represent thousands of hours of difficult work.

**Frederick:** Thanks, Grandpa! I can't wait to see them. I appreciate that you allowed me to conduct this interview, too!

**I.** Why does the author set the characters' names in boldface?

_____

**2.** What is the purpose of having some words set in regular font and some words set in italics?

_____

_____

**3.** Why do you think the author chose to present the text in this form, rather than using paragraphs and quotation marks?

_____

_____

_____

**4.** Why is Frederick interviewing Grandpa Davison?

_____

**5.** Complete the sentence below.

Grandpa Davidson's family moved from the city to the country because _____

_____ .

**6.** Write a short paragraph summarizing Grandpa Davidson's description of his youth.

_____

_____

_____

_____

_____

**7.** What relative would you most like to interview? Why?

_____

**8.** Write three questions that you would ask your relative in an interview.

1. _____

2. _____

3. _____

# Norman Rockwell

*How did Norman Rockwell's art reflect and affect American society?*

1  While looking at a photo of a Thanksgiving gathering, you might have heard a relative say that it looks "just like a Norman Rockwell painting." So who was Norman Rockwell? And what does he have to do with Thanksgiving pictures?

2  Norman Rockwell was born in New York City on February 3, 1894. He was the younger of two sons of a textile firm manager and his wife. Rockwell was interested in art early on, and he began art school at the age of fourteen. Later, he attended the National Academy of Design, before finishing his education at the Art Students League in New York City. While there, he created cover illustrations for several magazines for young men. These included *Boys' Life,* the magazine of the Boy Scouts of America.

3  At age 21, Rockwell and his own young family moved to New Rochelle, New York. This town was the home of many artists and illustrators. He continued producing work for magazines, including illustrations for *Life.* In 1916, the first Rockwell illustration appeared on a front cover of the *Saturday Evening Post.* During the next four decades, more than 300 issues of the magazine would feature his artwork. Many of his portrayals of life in the United States are still familiar to Americans today.

4  When the United States entered World War I, Rockwell wanted to serve his country in the military. He could not enlist because, despite being six feet tall, he weighed only 140 pounds. Rockwell did not give up so easily. He tried enlisting again after stuffing himself with calorie-rich foods. He finally gained enough weight to enlist. Rockwell was not sent abroad, though. Instead, he served as a military artist.

5  In 1920, Rockwell created illustrations for the first of many calendars he created for the Boy Scouts. For nearly the rest of his life, he would provide the art for each new calendar. In 1939, Rockwell was awarded the Boy Scouts' highest award given to adults: the Silver Beaver.

6  Rockwell is famous for creating art that made people smile. These works include portrayals of children visiting the dentist or getting a haircut.

He also created art featuring people at sporting events and gathered for holidays. Each year, people looked forward to the first April issue of the *Saturday Evening Post.* They wanted to see how many hidden "April Fool's" details they could find in his cover art.

7  Rockwell's art also reflected the more serious issues of the times. One example is *The Problem We All Live With,* created in 1964 at the height of the Civil Rights movement. The painting shows Ruby Bridges, a six-year-old African-American girl, as she is escorted to a formerly whites-only school. Just as it happened in real life, she is shown accompanied by four solemn U.S. marshals.

8  In 1943, Rockwell made a series of paintings called *Four Freedoms.* These four paintings were inspired by a speech given by President Franklin D. Roosevelt to Congress. They were reproduced on four consecutive covers of the Saturday Evening Post. These issues were an instant hit. Rockwell's cover paintings traveled across the United States to promote the sale of war bonds. They were a great success, raising $130 million for the war effort. The most famous of the *Four Freedoms* paintings is *Freedom from Want.* It shows a family gathered at a table for Thanksgiving, as Grandma serves a huge turkey.

9  In his final year of life, Rockwell received the highest honor America bestows on private citizens, the Presidential Medal of Freedom. He donated most of his art to a local historical society. These works formed the core of what is now the Norman Rockwell Museum in Stockbridge, Massachusetts. When he passed away in 1977, First Lady Rosalyn Carter attended his funeral. Norman Rockwell was considered by many as one of the greatest painters of the 20th century, but he humbly described himself as a "commercial illustrator."

**1.** Complete the timeline below by including a description of an event from Norman Rockwell's life that corresponds to each date. Refer to the text as needed.

1894: _____

1908: _____

1915: _____

1916: _____

1920: _____

1939: _____

1943: _____

1964: _____

1977: _____

**2.** Why did readers look forward to Rockwell's illustration for the first *Saturday Evening Post* of April each year?

_____

**3.** What influence did Norman Rockwell have on America during World War II? Cite evidence from the text in your answer.

_____

_____

_____

**4.** Explain why someone might look at a photograph of a Thanksgiving gathering and compare it to a Norman Rockwell painting.

_____

_____

**5.** What is *The Problem We All Live With* that Rockwell refers to in the title of his paining?

_____

**6.** Why was Rockwell awarded the Silver Beaver by the Boy Scouts?

_____

_____

# Trash or Treasure?

*Can something be valuable, even if it's not worth a lot of money?*

1   The garage door rattles loudly as Abigail rolls it up. Inside the dim garage, she can make out the shapes of boxes, bikes, lamps, chairs, and other assorted objects.

2   "Yikes! What a mess," Abigail says to herself. Grandma Louise is visiting friends in California, and Abigail has volunteered to help sort through the things in her grandmother's garage.

3   She walks up to one of the boxes and peeks inside to see the plain, colored spines of books without dust jackets. Another box contains neatly folded linens of various patterns: paisley, gingham, striped. Abigail spots a dusty tandem bike at the back corner of the garage, and a vague memory of her parents trying to ride it flashes through her mind.

4   With a sigh, she starts sorting the boxes, placing the ones that she thinks hold treasures on one side of the garage. The boxes that probably have mostly trash, she sets outside. A large, heavy box full of old sports equipment—badminton net, tennis rackets, a bat, a deflated basketball, and by the weight of it, maybe a bowling ball or two—takes Abigail a bit more effort to drag to the middle of the garage where she can sort through it better. When she looks back to where the box had been sitting, she sees a picture frame leaned against the wall, the backside of the frame facing her.

5   Abigail walks up to the frame and leans it forward to peek at the front. She expects it to be a poster or maybe an old photograph, but she's surprised to see a landscape painting. She turns the painting around to get a better look and sees that it depicts a snowy scene in a small New England town. Old cars are parked along the street, and light streams of smoke drift from each house's chimney. When Abigail's eyes travel down to the bottom right corner, she gasps.

6   "Norman Rockwell!" she shouts. Does her grandmother really have a Norman Rockwell painting stashed in her garage? Abigail's heart begins beating quickly. She knows enough about Rockwell to know that one of his paintings is worth a lot of money.

7   Abigail runs her hand lightly across the painting's surface. She wants to be sure it *is* a painting, and not a print. As her fingertips travel over the rough surface of brushstrokes, she's convinced. She carefully lifts the painting and carries it inside the house to do some research.

8   Abigail gets on her grandmother's computer to search online for *Norman Rockwell, painting, snow,* and *town,* and it doesn't take long to find information about the painting. Its title is *Stockbridge at Christmas,* and it's apparently well-known. *How in the world did Grandma end up with it?* Abigail wonders. *It must be worth a fortune if it's so famous!*

9   Abigail pulls out her phone and calls Grandma Louise. How could she have kept something so valuable in a dusty, cluttered garage?

10   When Grandma Louis answers, Abigail blurts out, "I found the painting!"

11   "What painting, honey?" Grandma Louise sounds confused.

12   "The Norman Rockwell!" says Abigail. "How long have you had it? *How* do you have it?"

13   "Normal Rockwell?" She still doesn't understand what Abigail is talking about. The line goes quiet for a few seconds, and then Grandma Louise bursts out laughing. "Oh, Abigail! Oh, I'm sorry you got so excited, but your grandpa painted that. It's a copy he made a long time ago when he used to paint for fun."

14   After getting off the phone, Abigail is surprised that she doesn't feel disappointed. "Maybe the painting isn't a real Rockwell," she thinks, "and maybe it's not worth a lot of money, but it's worth a lot to me because Grandpa painted it. This definitely goes in the treasure pile!"

As indicated, provide either a cause or an effect to complete each cause-and-effect relationship below. There may be more than one possible answer, but the cause or effect you provide must make sense according to events in the story.

**1. cause:** Abigail is asked to clean out her grandmother's garage.

**effect:** _____

**2. cause:** Abigail pulls a large box of sports equipment away from the wall.

**effect:** _____

**3. cause:** _____

**effect:** Abigail calls Grandma Louise.

**4. cause:** _____

**effect:** Abigail shouts, "Norman Rockwell!"

**5.** Provide your own example of a cause-and-effect relationship from the story.

**cause:** _____

**effect:** _____

**6.** Does this story take place in the past, present, or future? Explain your answer.

_____

_____

_____

_____

**7.** Why does Abigail decide the painting is still a "treasure," even though it is not a real Norman Rockwell painting?

_____

_____

**8.** What object is important and valuable to you, even though it may not have monetary value? What makes it valuable?

_____

_____

_____

_____

# Dining with the Stars

*How is dining in space different from eating on Earth?*

1    Spacesuits? Check! Oxygen? Check! Water? Check! Are we forgetting something? Food! If you send astronauts into space, you have to send along food as well. But what do astronauts eat, and how do they eat it?

2    Scientists take several factors into consideration as they plan meals for space. First, and possibly most important, is nutrition. Maintaining the astronauts' physical health is a top priority for any space mission. Astronauts must be fit in order to successfully work in the cramped, stressful conditions of a spacecraft's cabin. Providing junk foods to eat, such as potato chips, sodas, and pizza, would make the astronauts feel sluggish and unhealthy. Foods eaten in space need to be easily digestible, and most junk foods are not. No one wants belly problems in space—especially in tight quarters where everyone breathes the same, recycled air!

3    Variety and taste are also important. If the food that has been provided is unpalatable, then the astronauts may avoid eating it. If you've ever tried to concentrate on something important while your stomach growls, you'll know why the scientists in charge of a space mission want their astronauts to eat regularly. The important work performed in space can't be jeopardized by an astronaut daydreaming about delicious meals back on Earth.

4    The lack of gravity in a spacecraft also determines what foods can or cannot be eaten in space. Meals must be packaged carefully so they won't leak or spill into the cabin. Imagine the mess if a package of peas burst open, and hundreds of little green spheres began floating around! Foods that create too many crumbs are also avoided. The inside of a spacecraft is filled with equipment vital to a mission's success—as well as the astronauts' survival. Liquids or tiny bits of food could get inside a machine or electronic device and damage it. For the same reason, sharp utensils are never used onboard. A loose knife bouncing around inside the cabin would be dangerous.

5    Finally, weight is an important concern. The weight of every object included in a spacecraft must be calculated in order to ensure that there is enough fuel and power to carry the craft safely into space and home again. Food packaging is made to be as light as possible. Most foods are stored in vacuum-sealed plastic bags, and often, the foods are dehydrated. Removing the moisture from food and storing it in an airtight package allows the food to remain unrefrigerated for a long time without spoiling. When an astronaut is ready to eat, hot water is added to rehydrate the meal and warm it up.

6    Despite all these requirements, much of the food eaten in space is actually similar to what you might eat on any given day. Spaghetti with meat sauce, teriyaki beef, creamed spinach, scrambled eggs, waffles, granola bars, and nuts are just a small selection of what astronauts eat. Believe it or not, they also have fresh fruits and vegetables, at least for the first few days of a mission.

7    When it's time to eat, the foods—still in their packaging—are usually attached to trays. Then, the astronaut attaches the tray to a wall or across his or her lap. With everything anchored in place so the food can't get away, the meal is ready to begin.

8    Although nutrition and practicality are important things to consider, those in charge of planning meals also understand the role of psychology. While astronauts are in space, they are isolated from the rest of humanity, including their friends and families. Eating normal food—as normal as possible, anyway—can bring them comfort and a reminder of those who await their safe return to Earth.

**1.** Identify the sentence in the second paragraph that summarizes the main idea of text. Write it on the line below.

_____

**2.** What evidence does the author provide to support the main idea? Cite specific examples from the text in your answer.

_____

_____

_____

_____

_____

**3.** Which of the following is least likely to be supplied as a food choice for astronauts on a spacecraft? Place a checkmark on the line of the best answer.

_____ banana                       _____ canned soup

_____ pita chips                    _____ burrito

**4.** Which of the following is NOT described in the text as a consideration when determining which foods to bring on a space mission? Place a checkmark on the line of the correct answer.

_____ nutrition                     _____ weight

_____ cost                          _____ taste

**5.** Why are most of the meals sent into space first dehydrated and then vacuum-sealed in plastic packaging?

_____

_____

**6.** How does the lack of gravity in the spacecraft affect how foods are served?

_____

_____

_____

**7.** What is your favorite meal? Would it be available during spaceflight? Explain why or why not.

_____

_____

# NASA's Twin Mission

*How can studies in space help both astronauts and those on Earth?*

1    The National Aeronautics and Space Administration (NASA) will conduct a study of twins in space. This study is the first of its kind and will begin in March 2015. Scott Kelly, a veteran astronaut, will live aboard the International Space Station (ISS) for one year. At the conclusion of the study, Scott will have spent more consecutive time in space than any other American astronaut. Scott has been on long space missions in the past; one of his missions lasted six months.

2    Scott's twin brother Mark Kelly will stay on Earth. He will be an observational subject in the study. Mark can't be called a "control" subject, because his environment won't be controlled. He will be free to do what he would have done if he were not a participant in the study. Mark is a former astronaut who is married to Gabrielle Giffords, a former congresswoman. Mark retired to spend time with his wife after she was injured in a shooting. Mark and Scott Kelly are the only twins to have traveled in space.

3    Scott was the first person to wonder if his and his brother's experiences might be helpful in a study of twins. Scientists at the Human Research Program (HRP) at NASA considered his idea and agreed. The HRP decided to conduct ten separate studies on the twins. This study could compare the bodies of two brothers before, during, and after the ISS mission. Forty different institutions submitted proposals for studies. Eventually, the pool was narrowed down to ten. One and a half million dollars was made available to carry out the studies. NASA hopes that these studies will help them understand how living in space for an extended period of time impacts the bodies of humans.

4    NASA is focusing only on two people in these studies. Because there are not a large number of participants, the results of these experiments will not provide data as precise as most scientific studies. However, it will help scientists in the future when they do design studies that include more participants.

5    The study will focus on what happens to the twins at the molecular level. Scientists will collect blood samples from both men during different stages of the mission. The brothers will also take part in physical and psychological exams. One thing scientists will look at is the effect of living in space on human DNA. NASA also plans to study the effect of diet, lack of gravity, stress, and other factors. They will look at how these factors cause differences in the bacteria content in the blood, digestive system, and saliva. Another focus of the research will be studying how time spent in space affects decision making, alertness, perception, and reasoning.

6    NASA hopes to use the results to keep future space travelers healthy. This study will become very important as longer missions are planned in the future, such as a manned mission to Mars. When people eventually travel to Mars, they will most likely spend about three years in space to get there. The total amount of radiation these voyagers will be exposed to has never been experienced by space travelers before.

7    In addition to helping future astronauts and space travelers, NASA's twin study should help those living on Earth. Finding out how radiation and stress affect the chemical compounds in human cells should be useful in genetic studies. Exposure to similar stimuli takes place on Earth. NASA's twin mission will be helpful to scientists for decades to come.

**1.** Which of the following statements best summarizes the author's point of view? Place a checkmark on the line of the best answer.

_____ Because of radiation and other dangers, studying twins in space is a risky endeavor.

_____ Studying twins in space will result in research that benefits future astronauts as well as people on Earth.

_____ Mark and Scott Kelly are brave astronauts willing to put their lives in danger to benefit humankind.

_____ Mark will participate as an observational subject, but without a control subject, the results of the twin mission will not be very helpful.

**2.** Why are twins good candidates for a study on the effects of space travel?

_____

_____

**3.** Which of the following is NOT described in the text as a focus of the study? Place a checkmark on the line of the correct answer.

_____ the effects of space travel on DNA

_____ the maximum amount of time a human can survive in space

_____ the way bacteria in the body are affected by space travel

_____ psychological affects of living in space

**4.** Which of the following statements is true? Write **T** on the line of the true statement.

_____ Neither Mark nor Scott Kelly has traveled to space before.

_____ Mark has traveled to space in the past, but Scott has not.

_____ Scott has traveled to space in the past, but Mark has not.

_____ Both Scott and Mark Kelly have traveled to space before.

**5.** Why do you think NASA asks for a large number of proposals for studies, but then chooses only a small number of them to actually fund and complete?

_____

_____

**6.** Do you think a manned mission to Mars will occur in your lifetime? Why or why not?

_____

# An Out-of-this-World Summer

*What could you learn if you had the opportunity to attend space camp?*

1     Late Sunday afternoon, Jessica Brown and her parents arrive at the entrance to space camp in Huntsville, Alabama. A guide gives them a quick tour of the camp, and then the Browns walk their daughter to her dorm room, give her a quick hug, and wish her well. Jessica is nervous, but knows she has a week ahead of her that will be so busy, she'll hardly have time to miss her parents. When she meets her bunkmate, Jan, they discover they will be partners for the entire week. While Jessica is from nearby Florida, Jan has come all the way from Utah to attend the camp.

2     The first thing the girls do on Monday is view a three-dimensional film. It introduces them to the space program. In the afternoon, they learn about the many experiments being conducted in the zero-gravity environment of the International Space Station (ISS). Afterward, Jan and Jessica get to design a real biology experiment that scientists will evaluate and consider for conducting aboard the ISS in the future.

3     Tuesday's events are exhilarating. The girls strap into chairs and become immersed in an environment that simulates a visit to the moon. The pressure they feel is one-sixth of what they are used to. Jan is thrilled, but Jessica, while fascinated, is also a little uncomfortable at first because it is so unfamiliar to her. Eventually, she gets used to the environment. When they come out, she can definitely feel the stronger pull of Earth's gravity. Later the same day, the girls are exposed to a frictionless environment in a manned maneuvering unit.

4     On Wednesday, the space camp attendees spend a lot of time talking about manned missions to Mars. They discuss what it might be like to live on the planet. Different groups of campers discover the many requirements for colonization of the planet. Finally, all of the teams come together to explain how the planet might be colonized. Jessica and Jan decide that they admire those who would volunteer to be the first to colonize the planet, but that they themselves aren't particularly interested in this career path. Several of the space camp attendees are thrilled with the prospect of being among the first to live on the red planet.

5     Throughout the week, the girls partner with a few other members to design and build a rocket. They will actually launch it later in the week. This requires a lot of intellectual effort, and both Jan and Jessica are pleased that they have worked so hard in math class. They have to consider a lot of data while they build their rocket. They must also use math and physics to predict how their rocket will behave after it is launched.

6     Friday is the big day. All of the teams at space camp compete in the rocket-launch competition. Jessica and Jan's rocket performs as they predicted, but another rocket that is more streamlined and a little heavier wins the competition. The girls are not disappointed, though. They learned a ton about the physics of flight as they designed and launched their rocket. They are pleased with themselves for the knowledge they acquired and their accurate predictions.

7     On Saturday, Jessica's parents pick her up from camp. "What was your favorite thing that happened this week?" her father asks.

8     "I really enjoyed the astronaut simulators," Jessica says. "I really think I want to be an astronaut when I get older, and I am definitely interested in aeronautics. Next year, I think I would like to attend aviation camp!"

**I.** Is this story an example of realistic fiction? Why or why not?

_____

_____

_____

**2.** Which of the following is NOT an activity Jessica did at space camp? Place a checkmark on the line of the correct answer.

_____ watch a 3-D movie about the space program

_____ design, build, and launch a rocket

_____ ride in a machine that simulates what it feels like to be launched into space

_____ design a biology experiment that might be conducted on the ISS

**3.** Classify the following statements as **T** if a statement is true or **F** if a statement is false.

_____ Jessica loves experiencing what it feels like to be on the moon.

_____ Jessica's partner for the week is her dorm roommate, Jan.

_____ Neither Jessica nor Jan plan to visit Mars if the chance ever comes.

_____ Jan's rocket comes in first place at the launch competition, and Jessica feels disappointed that her rocket didn't win.

_____ Jessica would like to be an astronaut someday.

**4.** Why is Friday described as "the big day"?

_____

**5.** Why are Jan and Jessica glad they worked hard in math class?

_____

_____

**6.** Would you like to attend space camp? Why or why not?

_____

_____

**7.** Would you be willing to take part in a manned mission to Mars? Why or why not?

_____

_____

# Fire in the Sky

*What caused a massive, exploding fireball in the sky over Russia?*

1    On a cold February morning in 2013, just after dawn, the sky over the Russian province of Chelyabinsk erupted with a fireball brighter than the sun. The explosion could be seen for more than 50 miles in all directions. Powerful shock waves of energy rolled across the landscape. Windows shattered in thousands of buildings in six different cities. What would cause such as massive burst of fire and energy? Was Russia under attack?

2    The cause was not a bomb or anything else of human origin. It was the largest asteroid to enter Earth's atmosphere in more than 100 years. Scientists estimate that the Chelyabinsk asteroid measured about 65 feet in diameter and weighed as much as the Eiffel Tower. Traveling through space at around 40,000 miles per hour, the asteroid slammed into Earth's atmosphere. The intense friction produced an enormous amount of heat that destroyed the asteroid in a fiery explosion. Most of the material produced by the blast was gas and dust. Many smaller fragments fell to the ground as meteorites. Several weeks after the event, scientists retrieved a nearly one-ton chunk of meteorite from the bottom of a frozen lake. It was the largest piece of meteorite from the Chelyabinsk meteor that has yet been found.

3    Luckily, no one was killed in the blast, but nearly 1,500 people were injured. Most injuries were due to broken glass flying from shattered windows. People were also injured from falling due to the shock wave. Some people suffered eye strain or temporary blindness from the brightness of the fireball. Others suffered burns to the skin, similar to sunburn, due to the intensity of the light.

4    You may have noticed several words being used to describe the Chelyabinsk object: *asteroid, meteor, meteorite*. So which one is the correct term? In a way, they all are. It depends on where the object is and what you are describing. An *asteroid* is a small planet orbiting in our solar system. There are millions of asteroids. They vary in size from about ten yards wide to a few hundred miles wide. There are also much smaller objects travelling through space called *meteoroids*. Meteoroids range from the size of a grain of sand to about a meter across. When meteoroids enter Earth's atmosphere, they usually burn up and produce a flash or streak of light. The light is called a *meteor*. Asteroids also produce meteors when they burn in Earth's atmosphere. If any part of an asteroid or meteoroid survives the trip through Earth's atmosphere and falls to the ground, the piece of metal or rock is called a *meteorite*.

5    Although it is somewhat rare for asteroids to collide with Earth, it does happen. The largest impact in recorded history happened in Russia as well. In 1908, near the Tunguska River in a remote part of Siberia, an asteroid exploded a few miles above the ground. It wiped out tens of millions of trees across more than 800 square miles. The explosion is estimated to have been about 1,000 times more powerful than the atomic bomb dropped on Hiroshima, Japan. Because it happened so far from any population center, there were no known fatalities or injuries from the event.

6    A little more than 100 years passed between the Tunguska Event and the Chelyabinsk Meteor. Will it be another 100 years before the next asteroid collides with Earth? In order to make sure we know the answer, scientists try to monitor the skies for asteroids with orbits that could carry them toward Earth. However, it is a difficult task to locate and track asteroids. In the vastness of space, even an asteroid several miles wide is just a speck.

**I.** Classify each of the following statements by writing **O** if the statement is an opinion or **F** if the statement is a fact.

_____ The Tunguska Event was the most important scientific event in Russia during the 20th century.

_____ Most of the Chelyabinsk asteroid was destroyed when it exploded.

_____ Our solar system contains millions of asteroids that vary greatly in size.

_____ Meteor showers provide dazzlingly beautiful streaks of light across the night sky.

_____ Most likely, scientists will be unable to identify the next asteroid heading toward Earth.

_____ The Chelyabinsk asteroid was estimated to be about 65 feet in diameter.

**2.** What can you infer about the scientists who found the one-ton piece of meteorite or the work they did to retrieve it from the bottom of a frozen lake? Write your inference below.

_____

_____

**3.** Write a short paragraph comparing and contrasting asteroids, meteoroids, meteors, and meteorites.

_____

_____

_____

_____

_____

_____

**4.** Why did the asteroid explode in the atmosphere rather than smash into the ground?

_____

_____

**5.** Where does the Tunguska Event get its name? Place a checkmark on the correct answer below.

_____ The first scientist to write about the event was Dr. Ivan Tunguska.

_____ The asteroid exploded and destroyed a region near the Tunguska River.

_____ *Tunguska* is the Russian word for "asteroid."

# Dragon in Space

*What makes the* Dragon *spacecraft different from all previous spacecraft?*

1    The National Aeronautics and Space Administration, or NASA, was established in 1958 by the United States government. NASA's purpose is to develop and run the American space program. Since its founding more than 50 years ago, NASA has had some amazing success. The Apollo space mission carried the first humans to the moon in 1969. In the 1970s, Skylab was launched to become America's first space station. When *Atlantis* returned safely to Earth in 2011, it marked the end of 30 years and 135 missions for NASA's Space Shuttle program. And in the 1990s, NASA began working with the space programs of several other nations to build, maintain, and operate the International Space Station (ISS).

2    The *ISS* is an orbiting research laboratory. It allows scientists from around the world to conduct unique experiments in space. Where else could a researcher find an environment with almost no gravity? The scientists who live on the ISS usually spend about six months there before returning to Earth. Most of the time, the ISS has six people that are onboard running the station, but there have been as many as thirteen at once making the ISS their home. Of course, six months is a long time to be in space without access to a grocery store! Space vehicles are launched regularly to bring supplies and crew members to the space station.

3    During its final decade, one of the Space Shuttle program's missions was to transport supplies and crewmembers to and from the ISS. Space vehicles from other nations help with this task as well. However, every launch and landing of a space vehicle is extremely expensive. Until recently, all of NASA's space vehicles and missions were developed and paid for by the United States government. In 2005, plans were made to change the ways things had always been done.

4    NASA knew they would be ending the Space Shuttle program. So they started developing a new program for Commercial Resupply Services vehicles. CRS vehicles would be developed and operated by private companies, rather than the government. One of the goals was to reduce costs by having companies compete with each other. Each company made a plan for how they would build and launch their space vehicle—and what it would cost. NASA looked at the plans carefully, determining which one was the safest, most reliable, and also affordable.

5    In 2006, a private company called *SpaceX* won the contract. Work began right away to build their space capsule, called *Dragon.* The plan was to launch the unmanned *Dragon* into space atop a rocket. The *Dragon* capsule then detaches from the rocket and makes its way to the ISS. It attaches to the space station. The ISS crew retrieves their supplies. Then, the *Dragon* detaches from the ISS and heads back to Earth. It falls into the Pacific Ocean, and the capsule is recovered. Much of the material is reused to create a new *Dragon* capsule.

6    After several years of testing, the *Dragon* was finally ready for its first real mission. On October 8, 2012, the *Dragon* was launched on a rocket and, a few days later, completed its mission successfully. The ISS was safely resupplied, and the first commercial space vehicle was a reality. The *Dragon* completed a second successful mission in 2013. Today, SpaceX is working on a version of their space capsule that can carry a crew into space.

7    Although the *Dragon* was the first commercial space vehicle to be used by NASA, it is no longer the only one. In late 2013, the *Cygnus* spacecraft, built and operated by another company, completed a mission to the ISS as well. The era of commercial space flight has been launched!

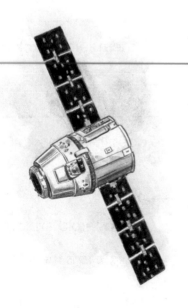

**I.** Why was the *Dragon* spacecraft different from all previous spacecraft launched into space?

_____

**2.** How many people usually live and work on the ISS at one time? Place a checkmark on the line of the best answer.

_____ 2                        _____ 12

_____ 6                        _____ 25

**3.** On average, how long does a crewmember spend aboard the ISS? Place a checkmark on the line of the best answer.

_____ one week           _____ six weeks

_____ one month        _____ six months

**4.** What is SpaceX? Place a checkmark on the line of the best answer.

_____ the second commercial spacecraft to supply the ISS

_____ a nickname for the ISS

_____ the company that built the *Dragon*

_____ America's first space station

**5.** Write out the words represented by each acronym.

ISS: _____

NASA: _____

CRS: _____

**6.** Why do you think the *Dragon* capsule lands in the Pacific Ocean? Provide at least two reasons.

_____

_____

_____

**7.** Provide one reason why commercial spacecraft might not be a good option for resupply missions.

_____

# Snowboarding 101

*What do the students in Terrence's class learn about snowboarding when a professional visits the class?*

1   The students in Mr. Peterson's classroom whispered to each other in excitement about the day's guest: professional snowboarder Lance Nichols. Anyone who had any interest in winter sports knew all about Lance Nichols' accomplishments in the last few years: medals at both the Winter X Games and the Winter Olympics, plus appearances in commercials and on sports shows. He was definitely the most famous speaker to ever address the class.

2   One student in particular was more excited about the visit than anyone else, but he didn't think of the guest as "Snowboarding Superstar Lance Nichols!" Terrence knew him as Uncle Lance. Terrence had emailed his uncle several months earlier to ask if he would be able to come speak to the class. Uncle Lance lived in Vermont, and he was always flying to the West or to Canada, or to even farther places around the world. The chance that he would be able to come was small, so Terrence was thrilled when his uncle emailed back and said he could make it.

3   Mr. Peterson began introducing the special guest. "You all know who's here today, so I'll just let him get started." The teacher waved toward the open door leading into the hallway. "Come on in, Lance."

4   Lance strode briskly into the classroom, carrying a snowboard and wearing a huge smile on his face. "Hey, everybody! How are you all doing this fine morning?"

5   Shouts of "Great!" and "Awesome!" came from around the room. Lance spotted his nephew toward the back of the class and gave him wink. Terrence smiled back, feeling proud to know someone who was so admired.

6   Lance gave a short history of snowboarding, explaining that it was a relatively new sport. "The first snowboards appeared about 100 years ago, but they were pretty primitive. They were just big planks of wood with a rope tied to the front. People would jump aboard, hold onto the rope, and try to steer themselves down a snowy hill using the rope. But then came the 'snurfer!'

That name's great, isn't it? In the '60s, a guy in Michigan tied two skis together, added a rope, and gave it to his daughters to play with. He called it the *snurfer* because it was kind of like a surfboard, but for snow. His girls loved cruising down the slopes on the snurfer, and so did their friends. He sold the idea to a big company, and they started making snurfers to sell. Snurfers were popular right away. Eventually, snowboard designs got better, with bindings added to help hold your feet onto the board."

7   Lance described how a lot of surfers and skateboarders took to snowboarding right away. "The way you balance and steer a snowboard is pretty similar to how you ride a surfboard or skateboard. If you lived someplace where there was no ocean, or it was too snowy to skateboard, but you liked those sports, then snowboarding was the perfect solution."

8   He told the class how snowboarding grew increasingly popular during the 1970s and 1980s, but it was banned at first from most ski resorts. "All those rowdy teenagers zipping around on their snowboards, right?" he laughed. "The ski resorts didn't want them disturbing the older, traditional skiers. But in the end, those first snowboarders became adults who still snowboarded, so the resorts changed their minds. Now, about 1 in every 3 people heading down the slope is riding on a snowboard."

9   Lance shared stories of his experiences in snowboarding competitions, both as an amateur and as a professional, and then he thanked the class for inviting him. The students applauded, and Lance signed autographs for a few minutes.

10   Terrence was one the few students who didn't rush to the front to get an autograph. He had the entire weekend ahead if he needed Uncle Lance to sign anything.

**1.** Authors often have more than one purpose for writing a text. Identify two purposes for this text by placing checkmarks on the lines of the two best choices.

_____ entertain          _____ inform

_____ convince          _____ explain

**2.** Write a sentence that summarizes the text.

_____

**3.** A *portmanteau* is a word created by combining two or more words into a single, new word. For example, *smog* is a portmanteau word that combines *smoke* and *fog*. What two words were combined to create the portmanteau word *snurfer*?

_____ and _____

**4.** Why were snowboarders banned early on from most ski resorts? Place a checkmark on the correct answer.

_____ Snowboards were considered unsafe to ride.

_____ Ski lifts were not designed to carry snowboarders up the slope.

_____ Snowboarders were mostly teenagers or children, and other skiers thought they were reckless.

_____ Snowboarders were mostly teenagers or children, and ski resorts did not believe they could afford to pay lift fees.

**5.** Why doesn't Terrence try to get Lance Nichols' autograph like the other students?

_____

_____

**6.** In your own words, explain how snowboarding is similar to riding a skateboard or a surfboard. How are they different?

_____

_____

_____

_____

**7.** Have you ever snowboarded? If you have, what did you like or dislike about it? If you have not, would like you like to someday? Why or why not?

_____

_____

# The X Games: A History

*What makes the sports of the X Games different from other sports?*

**1993:** The story of the X Games begins. Sports channel ESPN recognizes the increasing popularity of extreme sports. *Extreme sports* are loosely defined as those sports with lots of speed, height, and special equipment. Examples of extreme sports include skateboarding, mountain biking, bungee jumping, motocross motorcycles, and BMX dirt biking. Extreme sports are often seen as more dangerous than traditional sports. They are seldom included as parts of regular school athletic programs. ESPN chooses to create an international gathering of extreme sports enthusiasts. They will compete with each other for medals, similar to the tradition of the Olympics.

**1995:** After two years of development, the Extreme Games are held in June in Rhode Island and Vermont. Among the many competitions is skysurfing. In this sport, a skydiver jumps from a plane with a board attached to his or her feet. Then, he or she performs surfing- or skateboard-style tricks on the way down to the ground. Street luge was also featured. In this sport, the rider lies down on a huge skateboard and rolls downhill at speeds up to 90 miles per hour. Many of the games involved judges scoring athletes for their skills, rather than having them race to a finish line. This is similar to ice skating or gymnastics. For example, in freestyle BMX dirt biking, a rider performs tricks. The tricks may include flips, wheelies, balancing, and grinds. A grind is when the rider slides part of the bike along a ramp's edge or a railing. Several hundred thousand people attend the first Extreme Games. The event is considered a huge success, and plans are made to hold another competition the next year.

**1996:** The Extreme Games are renamed the X Games. Once again, the competition is held in Rhode Island, and it is as well-attended as the first games. At a special press conference, ESPN announces that the first Winter X Games will be held during the next winter.

**1997:** In late January, the first Winter X Games are held in Big Bear Lake, California. Events included snowboarding and freestyle skiing. Although attendance is much smaller at the winter event, it is still considered a success. Plans are made to hold Winter X Games each year, along with the regular X Games planned for each summer.

**1998–2002:** The X Games and Winter X Games continue to grow in popularity. They are televised to millions of viewers around the world. The games become a showplace for new tricks in skateboarding, snowboarding, and other extreme sports. Amateurs around the world begin dreaming of the day they can become good enough to compete with the best in their sport. In fact, so many competitors hope to be part of the official X Games, the organizers begin holding qualifying competitions. Qualifying events are held throughout the year in different cities around the United States. The best athletes from these qualifying events are then invited to compete in the X Games. In 2002, the Winter X Games are held in Aspen, Colorado, for the first time. Aspen becomes the permanent home for all future Winter X Games.

**2003–Present:** In 2003, the X Games are held in Los Angeles, and LA becomes the permanent home for all future X Games. In 2013, special international X Games events are held in Brazil, Spain, and Germany, and a Winter X Games event is held in France.

**1.** Classify the following statements as **T** if a statement is true or **F** if a statement is false.

_____ The *X* in X Games stands for *Exciting.*

_____ For more than a decade, the X Games have been held in Los Angeles, California.

_____ As long as an athlete is a professional in a sport featured at the X Games, he or she can be part of the competition.

_____ The first X Games were held in Aspen, Colorado, in 1993.

_____ From the very beginning, sports channel ESPN has played a major role in both the X Games and the Winter X Games.

_____ In general, more people attend the Winter X Games than the X Games held each summer.

_____ The X Games were popular right from the start.

**2.** Which event is NOT referred to in the text as a past or current X Games event? Place a checkmark on the correct answer.

_____ skateboard racing          _____ freestyle BMX

_____ skysurfing                         _____ street luge

**3.** Why did the X Games organizers create qualifying events? What purpose do qualifying events serve?

_____

_____

_____

**4.** The information in the text is organized in blocks of text corresponding to each year or span of years in the X Games' history. Why do you think the author chose to organize the text this way? Do you think this was or was not a good way to organize the information? Explain your answer.

_____

_____

_____

_____

_____

_____

# A Birthday to Remember

*How can sharing hobbies bring people together?*

1   Gabriela glimpsed up at the bright, blue sky, and drank in the fresh air of a warm, sunny day in Los Angeles. Although she was born here, Gabriela had not been back to visit since she was three years old. That was when her parents had divorced, and Gabriela's mother moved with her and her siblings to Indiana. To celebrate Gabriela's thirteenth birthday, her grandparents had flown her back to visit with them in Los Angeles. Now, on the third day of her visit, Gabriela was spending the whole day with her father.

2   Gabriela walked through her father's house, admiring the artwork hanging throughout the rooms. As a professional tour guide, he had spent many years working with a company that hosted birding trips around the world. He had visited an amazing number of beautiful places. Over the years, Gabriela's father had sent her original artwork from his trips, and she proudly displayed them in her bedroom.

3   Gabriela stopped in her tracks when she noticed a watercolor of a person climbing a huge slab of limestone. "Dad, did you paint this one?" He nodded, and Gabriela continued, "Seeing this makes me miss my climbing team back home. I can't remember if I told you, but I started indoor rock wall climbing. Just last week, I finally finished a 5.11b climb!"

4   Gabriela's father smiled, slightly surprised. "Gabby, if you'd prefer to climb today, we can do that instead of bird watching. I have a membership with the local climbing gym. If you didn't bring your shoes and harness, that's no problem, because we can rent those at the gym."

5   "I can't believe you're a rock climber too, Dad! I can't wait to show you how I'm working on bouldering problems!" Gabriela bounded to the guestroom and grabbed her shoes and purse. "I'm bringing my binoculars though, in case we still have time afterward to drive to the Ballona Wetlands to watch birds."

6   Not long afterward, the pair arrived at the climbing gym. It was the gym's policy for all first-time guests to take Climbing 101, so Gabriela quickly completed the short course and became belay-certified for the gym. Then, she joined her father at the bouldering wall. She noticed that he was struggling on a VB route. After he fell onto the mat below, he joined Gabriela on the bench nearby. "I've been top rope climbing for about two years now. To get stronger, I started bouldering just a few months ago. I'm still working on beginner-level routes, and this one is giving me fits. Any advice for your old man?" he asked Gabriela.

7   She studied the sequence in the bouldering route he just completed. Gabriela noticed where her father might benefit from a different technique. "Yeah, I think it'll be easiest if I try it first to see how I do," she said. They both watched each climber take a turn on the bouldering wall. When there was a lull, Gabriela hopped up to the route. She put her hands on the start holds, and easily completed the route. She turned back toward her father, saying, "Okay, Dad—I'm going to climb that one again. I want you to pay attention to my feet."

8   Gabriela's father watched her feet carefully as she completed the route. She sat back down next to her father, smiling. "See, I think if you flag your foot to the left as you reach for that blue jug," she said, "you'll maintain better balance."

9   After another hour of climbing, Gabriela and her father decided to drive to the wetlands to do a bit of bird watching at sunset. This would be a birthday trip that Gabriela would remember!

**1.** Is this story fiction or nonfiction? How do you know?

_____

_____

**2.** Gabriela is excited to tell her father about finishing a "5.11b climb." Based on the context of how it is used in the story, what does 5.11b most likely refer to? Place a checkmark on the line of the best choice.

_____ cost                                    _____ location

_____ difficulty                              _____ minimum age

**3.** Based on information from the text, which of the following best describes Gabriela's relationship with her father? Place a checkmark on the line of the best choice.

_____ Gabriela visits him once a year in Los Angeles.

_____ Gabriela has not seen or spoken with him in many years.

_____ Gabriela doesn't see her father often, but they have a good relationship.

_____ Gabriela lives with her father in Los Angeles.

**4.** Why do you think the gym requires all first-time visitors to take a basic climbing class, even if they have experience climbing at others gyms?

_____

_____

**5.** Write two words that describe Gabriela's father. Cite evidence from the story to support your choices.

_____ : _____

_____ : _____

**6.** *Lingo* is the special words used for specific activities or by those who are involved in a specific activity. Why do you think the author chose to include rock climbing lingo in the text, such as *bouldering, VB, jug,* and *flag*?

_____

_____

**7.** What activities are you involved in that require special skills? Does the activity have lingo used by participants? Provide some examples of the lingo.

_____

_____

# The Multifaceted Shaun White

*What are the talents and interests of Olympic gold medalist Shaun White?*

1   Shaun White was born in 1986 in San Diego, California. Before he was even one year old, White had to have two surgeries to correct a heart defect, but this rough start wasn't going to slow him down. As he grew, White wouldn't let anything keep him from being an active participant in sports. He began skiing when he was just four years old. His mom thought she might be able to slow him down if she gave him a snowboard instead. White just started going faster! Even at such a young age, people were aware of how good of an athlete he was.

2   In the summertime, White started skateboarding, and no one was surprised that he excelled at it. Professional skateboarder Tony Hawk became aware of White's talent, and he began mentoring the young skater. Hawk helped White become a pro skateboarder when he was only seventeen. People called White the "Flying Tomato" because of the heights he reached and his bright red hair.

3   Snowboarding became a Winter Olympic sport in 1998. At the Winter Olympics of 2006, White won his first gold medal in the snowboarding half-pipe event. In this event, snowboarders perform intricate tricks on a snow-covered surface that looks like a pipe cut in half horizontally. Snowboarding participants are awarded points based on the difficulty of the tricks they attempt and how well they do them. White won another gold medal in the same event in 2010. He completed many tricks that no one had done before. He also completed tricks that no else has ever done since! When he failed to medal in the Winter Olympic Games in 2014, many people were impressed by how graciously he handled his fourth-place finish.

4   At the Winter X Games, White competes in snowboarding. Then, when the weather gets warm, he competes at the Summer X Games in skateboarding events. He most recently won a gold medal in 2011 in Los Angeles in the X Game vert event. In this event, skateboarders skate up and down a vertical ramp and perform tricks.

5   White is one of the world's most popular snowboarders, so he has a snowboarding video game named after him. But he is also such a good skateboarder, he has his own skateboarding video game, too. This game is one of many products White has been signed to endorse. Others include an action sport clothing line with his name on it. He is also a partner with companies that produce sunglasses and outerwear. White has been promoting products since he was six years old.

6   One of his newest endeavors is playing guitar in a band called *Bad Things*. They played at the 2013 Lollapalooza music festival and released their first album in 2014. White likes being a member of a larger group, and he tries to make sure they are not known as "Shaun White's band." Still, since he is the most famous member, people tend to call them that. Bad Things has appeared on many television programs, including the Tonight Show. White likes the anonymity of being in the band, because, despite his fame, sometimes he is not recognized. When he competed, he often wore his fiery red hair long. Now, he keeps it shorter, and that helps to protect his privacy when he is in public.

7   White is a talented athlete who reached the pinnacle of his sport, but he maintains other interests as well. As his athletic career winds down, his future is still bright because of his savvy business sense. White enjoys life and has a good group of friends—and bandmates—to share it with.

**1.** Complete the lines below by including a description of an event from Shaun White's life that corresponds to each date. Refer to the text as needed.

1986: _____

1990: _____

2006: _____

2011: _____

2014: _____

**2.** Why was Shaun White nicknamed the "Flying Tomato"?

_____

**3.** Shaun White has excelled at two sports in particular. What are they?

_____     _____

**4.** Which of the following statements is true? Place a checkmark on the line of the correct answer.

_____ Shaun White has won gold medals at both the Summer and Winter Olympics.

_____ Shaun White has won a gold medal at each Olympics in which he competed.

_____ Shaun White has won gold medals at two different Winter Olympics.

_____ Shaun White has won gold medals at the Summer and Winter X Games, but not for any Olympic events.

**5.** What is Shaun White's role in the band Bad Things? Place a checkmark on the line of the correct answer.

_____ drummer         _____ guitarist

_____ manager         _____ lead singer

**6.** What is the author's opinion of Shaun White? Cite evidence from the text to support your answer.

_____

_____

**7.** Do you have a favorite athlete or famous person you admire? What do you admire about this person?

_____

_____

# Parking Lot Plans

*What is Sophia's big idea, and why are all the skaters so excited about it?*

1 Sophia rolled over to the edge of the parking lot, got off her skateboard, and sat on the concrete curb. For half an hour, she had been practicing ollies, but she just couldn't get her right foot to slide the way it was supposed to. Instead of catching air, the front end of her board kept slamming back to the ground, and a couple of times she had lost her balance and stumbled forward off the deck. With so many great skaters zipping around, doing all kinds of tricks and making everything look easy, Sophia needed a break.

2 The old parking lot had become a magnet for the neighborhood kids who liked to skate, even though it was mostly just a flat surface. At least no one hassled them here. The other places nearby where they had tried to skate were off-limits, and the few times they had tried, the business owners would come out and yell at them. One even called the police. No one seemed to care about the abandoned parking lot, so even if it wasn't perfect, it was the place they all went for skateboarding.

3 Sophia watched her friend Braxton doing kickflips, and then he did a tailslide down the length of a low concrete barrier separating two sections of the lot. *He's so good!* thought Sophia. *Too bad he doesn't have a better place to practice.* And then she had an idea.

4 "Braxton!" yelled Sophia, and she waved at him to come over.

5 Braxton rolled to where she sat and asked, "What's up?"

6 She explained her idea, and Braxton nodded excitedly. Soon, he had all the other skaters gathered around them, and Sophia shared her plan. She added, "We'll all need to work together. The more parents and business owners that we can get involved, the more chance we have of pulling this off."

7 For the next two weeks, Sophia, Braxton, and the others worked hard to put the plan into action. Each of them had spoken with his or her parents about the empty lot and what they hoped could be done with it. In teams of twos, the skaters had also walked door-to-door, visiting the businesses that didn't like skateboarders hanging around near their storefronts. They explained the plan and how it would benefit the businesses.

8 Sophia had printed copies of a one-page sheet detailing their plan, including a date when they could address members of the city council. They passed out the flyer to everyone they spoke with. They encouraged anyone who could make it to attend the city council meeting.

9 When the date finally arrived, Sophia couldn't believe the turnout at city council chambers. She recognized many of her friends' parents, and at least half the business owners they spoke with were there, too.

10 At last, Sophia could share her idea with the people who could make it real.

11 "Good evening, council members," Sophia began. "As a young person who enjoys skateboarding, the options for where I can skateboard are severely limited. As my friends and I have discovered, we are unwelcome along most of the sidewalks near our homes, especially wherever there are businesses. In the end, the empty parking lot on Charles Avenue has become the only place we have to skate. Most of the skaters will tell you that it's not an ideal place to skate, and my guess is that some of the parents will argue that it isn't a *safe* place to skate. I propose that the lot be purchased by the city and renovated to be the city's first skate park."

12 For the next hour, parents and business owners took turns explaining their support for Sophia's idea. When a vote was taken, the council approved the skate park, 7–2. Sophia and the other skaters cheered. The abandoned parking lot would soon become a well-maintained skate park!

**1.** What are the two main settings in this story?

_____ and _____

**2.** What is the conflict in this story?

_____

_____

**3.** How is the conflict resolved?

_____

_____

**4.** Authors include specific details when they write in order to make a story more interesting and believable. Identify two specific details from the story, and explain how they make the story more interesting or believable.

_____

_____

_____

**5.** A *win-win situation* is when everyone involved benefits from results. How is the building of the skate park an example of a win-win situation?

_____

_____

_____

**6.** If the other skaters had chosen not to help, do you think Sophia and Braxton would have succeeded with the skate park plan? Explain your answer.

_____

_____

_____

**7.** Describe a time when you were part of group working toward a common goal. What was your role? Would the goal have been achieved without everyone's help?

_____

_____

_____

_____

# America's First Railroad

*Why was the Baltimore & Ohio Railroad so important to 19th century America?*

1    It was the Fourth of July, 1828. The last surviving signer of the Declaration of Independence, 90-year-old Charles Carroll, was on hand as part of a ceremony to mark the beginning of a new business venture. He was honored to lay the first stone of what would become America's most important railway of the 19th century: the Baltimore & Ohio Railroad.

2    Baltimore, Maryland, was one of several major seaports along America's east coast, but it had one advantage over the others. Baltimore sat farthest inland, so it was naturally closer to the new cities, states, and territories being added to the increasingly larger nation of the United States. Trains rolling along tracks were a new idea at the time, but it was clear that railroads would be the transportation choice of the future. So, business leaders in Baltimore began planning a railroad to link Baltimore with points farther west. They hoped, eventually, to run tracks all the way to the Ohio River. In turn, they would make Baltimore the most important city in the east.

3    The first stretch of track was completed by 1830. It was not terribly long, reaching Ellicott's Mills, Maryland, which was just 13 miles away. However, the trains that would travel this line of track would be made available to the public. Not for free, of course, but this railroad would be the first to carry paying passengers and to ship goods for the public.

4    America's first steam locomotive, nicknamed "Tom Thumb," pulled the first train car along the new run of track to test it out. But then a train car pulled by horses made the same trip, and the horse-drawn train was faster! So at the beginning, the trains of the Baltimore & Ohio Railroad were powered by horses. Within just a few years, though, steam-powered locomotives took over for good. They became the main source of long-distance transportation across America during the 1800s.

5    After that first short stretch of track was completed, work continued quickly to extend the railroad farther west. Tracks followed major rivers through Maryland, and then they crossed the Potomac River into Virginia. In 1853, the *Ohio* part of the B&O Railroad's name finally became a reality. The line reached the Ohio River at the city of Wheeling, West Virginia. A track 380-miles long now ran from Baltimore to the Ohio River.

6    The B&O Railroad was a huge financial success. A strong transportation system was vital to the growing nation. The railroad supplied people and materials to the inner areas of the young country. It moved them quickly and safely. Baltimore, as the owners had hoped, became one of the richest cities in America.

7    Then came the Civil War. During the war, the rail line was used to supply Union troops with food and arms. However, much of the track ran through Confederate territory. This fact made the railroad difficult to defend. Raids on trains carrying supplies were common. Many historians believe the Civil War lasted longer because the railroad was so vulnerable to attacks. If the Union had gotten all of its supplies without interference, the Confederate armies would have been defeated sooner.

8    After the war, the tracks were repaired, and the B&O Railroad continued to grow. By the 1870s, tracks stretched from Baltimore all the way to Chicago, Illinois. However, the company began suffering financial difficulties. It had spent a lot of money on repairs after the war, and even more to expand its services. As the 19th century closed, the B&O Railroad went bankrupt. In 1901, another company bought most of The Baltimore & Ohio Railroad. The B&O continued operating under its name until the 1980s. Then, further purchases by other companies finally put the name to rest, and the Baltimore & Ohio Railroad was no more.

**NAME** _____

**1.** Where did the Baltimore & Ohio Railroad get its name? Place a checkmark on the line of the correct answer.

_____ The railroad was founded by businessmen from Baltimore and Ohio.

_____ The first steam engines were manufactured in Baltimore and Ohio.

_____ The railroad ran from Baltimore to the Ohio River.

_____ The railroad was found by Charles Baltimore and Nicholas Ohio.

**2.** Why was Baltimore considered a good location to start a railroad company?

_____

_____

**3.** Complete the sentence below.

"Tom Thumb" was the nickname of _____ .

**4.** Describe the impact of the Civil War on the B&O Railroad.

_____

_____

_____

**5.** Even though steam engines were available when the B&O Railroad began operating, the first trains were pulled by horses. Why?

_____

_____

**6.** Place checkmark on the line of the answer that best completes the sentence.

The 19ᵗʰ century refers to the _____ .

_____ 1700s        _____ 1900s

_____ 1800s        _____ 2000s

**7.** The author writes that steam locomotives were the main source of long-distance travel in the 1800s. What mode of transportation do you think became the main source of long-distance travel in the 1900s? Explain your answer.

_____

_____

_____

# A Basement Full of Trains

*Can a model train set help Jeremiah get to know his grandfather better?*

1    Jeremiah followed Grandpa Watkins down the steep stairs into the basement. When his grandfather had said, "Come on, I want to show you something," Jeremiah suspected it would have something to do with toy trains. He didn't know a whole lot about his grandfather, but he had heard that toy trains were Grandpa Watkins' hobby. To be polite, Jeremiah had agreed to go see what his grandfather wanted to show him, but he thought it was kind of silly for a grown-up to play with toy trains. He hadn't played with toys like that since he was little, when he had a few Thomas the Tank Engine trains and some wooden tracks.

2    Jeremiah didn't know his Grandpa and Grandma Watkins very well. They had visited a few times over the years, but this trip was the first time he had ever been to their home. After spending the previous day driving in the car, Jeremiah and his family had arrived really late the night before. Grandpa and Grandma Watkins welcomed them with hugs and kisses, but once all the bags were brought in, everybody had gone right to bed.

3    This morning, they had all eaten a big breakfast together, cooked by his mom and Grandma Watkins, and talked a bit about their lives. Jeremiah answered a lot of questions about school, his friends, and what he liked to do, but the whole conversation had seemed kind of stiff. His grandparents were close relatives, but he felt unsure about how he should act. Could he be goofy and laid-back, like he was around his friends and family, or should he be more formal and respectful, like he would act around adults at church or school?

4    When Jeremiah and his grandfather got to the bottom of the stairs, most of the basement was too dark to see much of anything. Grandpa Watkins placed his hand on the light switch, turned to Jeremiah, and asked, "Are you ready?" He wiggled his eyebrows up and down and gave Jeremiah a goofy smile. Jeremiah couldn't help himself, and he started to laugh.

5    "Sure, let's see what you got going on down here."

6    Grandpa Watkins flipped on the light, and Jeremiah's own eyebrows rose up toward his forehead. He couldn't believe what he saw. A gigantic table filled nearly the entire basement, and on top of the table was a little world of mountains, lakes, buildings, and, as he had predicted, trains and train tracks. The tracks wound around the table in all sorts of configurations. They crossed bridges, tunneled through mountains, snaked around lakes, and traveled between rows of little buildings. Jeremiah understood immediately the amount of work that must have gone into building the model.

7    "Holy smokes!" Jeremiah exclaimed. "You built all this?"

8    "Most of it, sure," Grandpa Watkins said with a chuckle. "A lot of the little details are things I bought at a store or ordered online, like the little buildings, the trees, some of the bridges. But I did design the whole thing and put it together. The mountains are sculpted out of wood and chicken wire and covered with glue and paper, like papier-mâché. I added the grass and trees and all that. You're looking at a few years of work here."

9    Jeremiah walked slowly around the perimeter of the basement, admiring all the little details of the model. Everything looked so realistic, except it was all tiny. There were even miniature people scattered across the landscape.

10    "Do you want to fire it up?" Grandpa Watkins asked, and he pointed to a series of switches and levers along one side of the table. "This is where we control all the trains. Pick one of the engines, and I'll show you how it's done."

11    Jeremiah and his grandfather spent the rest of the morning playing with toy trains, and Jeremiah had to admit: he didn't feel one bit silly about it.

**I.** Which of the following best describes Jeremiah's relationship with Grandpa Watkins? Place a checkmark on the line of the best answer.

_____ Jeremiah is meeting his grandfather for the first time.

_____ Jeremiah has met his grandfather a few times in the past, but they don't know each other very well.

_____ Jeremiah and his grandfather have a very close relationship and spend a lot of time together.

_____ Jeremiah lives with Grandpa and Grandma Watkins.

**2.** Who else from Jeremiah's family has come along for the visit to his grandparent's home? Place a checkmark on the correct answer.

_____ his mother and father                    _____ his mother, sister, and brother

_____ his mother, father, sister, and brother                    _____ The story does not say.

**3.** Why is Jeremiah surprised when Grandpa Watkins turns on the lights?

_____

**4.** What do you think impressed Jeremiah the most about the model train set? Explain your answer.

_____

_____

_____

**5.** Why does Jeremiah feel uncomfortable during breakfast? Do you think he feels the same way at the end of the story? Explain your answer.

_____

_____

_____

**6.** Make a prediction about the future of Jeremiah's relationship with his grandfather.

_____

_____

_____

_____

# The Legend of John Henry

*In the battle of a man versus a machine, does the man stand a chance?*

1   Let's go back to a time when thousands of men worked from first light to final dark, breaking rocks, digging ditches, and laying long, twin lines of steel rail over the prairie, across deserts, and right through mountains.

2   We arrive at a temporary camp set up at the base of a mountain. Sometime during the night, a strange contraption was delivered to the camp. When the men wake and crawl wearily from their tents, they see Mr. Boss leaning against it, a grin stretched tightly across his weather-beaten face.

3   "Whadya think, boys?" asks Mr. Boss. "We got this here drilling machine courtesy of the company men back east. It's gonna cut through that mountain in no time."

4   The men had been working for months, chipping a tunnel through the mountain. The work was exhausting, and at times the task seemed impossible, but little by little they had progressed. Each man was proud of the work he'd done, but they all knew who deserved the most credit: John Henry. He was the most enormous man any of them had ever seen, and they were sure he was the hardest-working man any of them would meet in their lifetimes.

5   Mr. Boss continues: "This here machine can do as much work in a couple hours as a dozen men working all day."

6   "That machine won't replace me," says John Henry calmly.

7   Mr. Boss laughs. "Oh, John Henry, there's no doubt you're strong as a dozen men, but you're still no match for a machine."

8   John Henry is quiet for a moment before he says, "Let's find out."

9   For months, the men have watched John Henry swinging a steel hammer in each hand and wrecking rocks for hours on end. If any human being alive could beat that machine, John Henry was the one.

10   "Suits me fine, John Henry. Man versus machine! We'll have a race at noon, see who can dig the most in two hours time."

11   At noon, the drilling machine chugs away at the base of the mountain, while John Henry stands several yards away, slowly and quietly lifting each hammer in turn.

12   Then, Mr. Boss yells, "Dig!"

13   The drilling machine leaps at the rock, its rotating tip grinding against stone. John Henry hammers blow after blow, stone chips bouncing off his body and scattering across the ground.

14   John Henry and the machine eat away at the mountain, inch-by-inch, foot-by-foot, tunneling their way through solid stone. Sweat pours off John Henry's back and drips silently to the ground, while the high-pitched whine of the drilling machine echoes through the camp.

15   No one had ever seen John Henry work like this before, and a few of the men begin to worry. How can he keep going? But instead of slowing down, John Henry smashes stone even harder, even faster, and rock explodes from the hole.

16   When Mr. Boss finally yells "Time's up!" the winner is clear; John Henry has dug a tunnel almost twice as long as the machine. The men throw their hats in the air and set up whooping and hollering. John Henry beat the machine!

17   But then they all watch, as if in slow motion, as John Henry collapses to the ground. He is no more, and the victory of man over machine is short-lived.

18   Later that day, the men lay their friend to rest, while the sound of a far-off drill mingles with their last words for John Henry.

**I.** Which of the following best describes the theme of the John Henry tale? Place a checkmark on the line of the best answer choice.

_____ A human being's desire to work hard and succeed is stronger than a machine.

_____ Someday, all human labor will be replaced by machines, and it is a losing battle to fight against this fact.

_____ The owners of railroad companies wanted to see progress, no matter what the cost.

_____ Each of us succeeds or fails on our own, and others will seldom step forward to help.

**2.** Who is the protagonist in the story? _____

**3.** Who is the antagonist in the story? _____

**4.** What is the conflict in the story? _____

_____

_____

**5.** Which part of the story is the climax? Place a checkmark on the line of the correct answer.

_____ when John Henry dies                    _____ when John Henry accepts the challenge to race

_____ when John Henry wins the race            _____ when the machine arrives

**6.** Is this a realistic story or a fantasy? Explain your answer.

_____

_____

_____

**7.** Imagine a retelling of this story as if it took place now. How would it be different? What would the machine be? What job would the John Henry character have? Would the outcome be the same? Describe what you imagine on the lines below.

_____

_____

_____

_____

_____

# "The Beatles!"

*Who were The Beatles, and what was Beatlemania?*

1   The story of The Beatles begins in Liverpool, England, in 1957, when teenager John Lennon received a cheap guitar from his mother. He quickly learned to play and soon formed a band called the *Quarrymen* with a few of his classmates. Lennon was a fan of the new rock-and-roll style of music coming from America. He loved Elvis Presley, Buddy Holly, and Little Richard. So, he convinced the Quarrymen to play rock and roll songs, and Lennon started wearing jeans and a leather jacket.

2   At the *Quarrymen's* second live show, Lennon met Paul McCartney, a student from another school, and invited him to join the band. Paul's friend, 14-year-old George Harrison, came onboard next. For the next few years, other band members came and went, but the trio of John, Paul, and George remained strong. The *Quarrymen* eventually changed their name, first to The Silver Beetles, and then just The Beatles.

3   As they played more live shows around Liverpool, The Beatles' reputation grew. Audiences loved the music, but The Beatles were also known for their goofy stage antics. Lennon in particular entertained audiences with funny voices, puns and jokes, and wild antics onstage. Their popularity soon grew beyond Liverpool. In 1960, The Beatles were invited to Hamburg, Germany, for a month-long series of shows. They would return to Hamburg again in 1961 and 1962. While they played there, they met drummer Richard Starkey, who went by the stage name Ringo Starr. He became a good friend of the band and would later become a Beatle as well.

4   In 1962, record-store owner Brian Epstein convinced The Beatles to take him on as their manager. He encouraged them to change their image from leather-clad rock and rollers to something more professional. The Beatles were soon performing in matching suits. Epstein also got the band into the recording studio. The Beatles had mostly been playing cover versions of other people's music. However, both Lennon and McCartney had been hard at work writing their own songs as well. The original songs would serve as their first recordings.

5   When they entered the studio to cut their first single, producer George Martin insisted they needed a great drummer. Immediately, the guys knew who they wanted: Ringo Starr. And so with their first single, "Love Me Do," the quartet of John, Paul, George, and Ringo was set.

6   The Beatles arrived at a perfect moment in pop music history. The initial wave of excitement created by the birth of rock and roll in the mid-1950s had worn off. Teens around the world were looking for "the next big thing." With their matching suits, incredibly catchy songs, and witty personalities, The Beatles were it. Throughout 1963, their singles and albums topped the charts in Britain, and Beatlemania was born. Wherever the band went, they were greeted by hundreds, sometimes thousands, of screaming fans hoping to get a glimpse of the lovable moptops (a reference to their shaggy hairstyles).

7   By the time The Beatles arrived in the United States in February 1964, American teenagers were already swept up in the music and fun of Beatlemania. When The Beatles performed live on television a few days later, nearly 75 million people watched.

8   For the next six years, The Beatles ruled the music world. Their singles and albums sold many millions of copies, and they made several popular films, but they also reflected the great cultural changes of the late-1960s. Their hair grew much longer, their music became heavier and more experimental, and they explored different spiritual and political ideas. By the time the band finally called it quits in 1970, it was clear that The Beatles had been something special.

**1.** Draw a line from each band member's first name to his last name.

John                    Harrison

Paul                    Starr

George                  McCartney

Ringo                   Lennon

**2.** Write a sentence to summarize each paragraph of the text.

1. _____

2. _____

3. _____

4. _____

5. _____

6. _____

7. _____

8. _____

**3.** Classify the following statements as **T** if a statement is true or **F** if a statement is false.

_____ The Silver Beetles first formed in Hamburg, Germany, in the late-1950s.

_____ John Lennon loved American rock and roll music.

_____ Ringo Starr's real name is Richard Starkey.

_____ Beatlemania was born when The Beatles toured America in 1964.

_____ Before joining the Beatles, Paul McCartney had his own band called The Quarrymen.

_____ The Beatles manager got them to wear matching suits when they played.

**4.** If The Beatles were a band today, how would their story be different? How would it be the same? Be specific.

_____

_____

_____

_____

# Mackenzie and The Racket

*How will Mackenzie's nerves affect her first time singing with the band?*

1    Mackenzie's feet felt heavier with each step she took as she walked reluctantly up the long driveway. She had predicted she might feel nervous today, but the way her stomach flipped and flopped surprised her. The driveway curved at the top of the hill, so she couldn't see into the garage, but she clearly heard the loud *kerrrrrang!* of an electric guitar and a few quick, sharp beats and a big cymbal crash on a drum set. Mackenzie inhaled deeply, told herself to be brave, and then rounded the curve.

2    Cameron was fiddling with the knobs on an electric guitar dangling from his shoulders. He looked up and said, "Mackenzie! Awesome, you're here! You know everybody else, right?"

3    "Sure," answered Mackenzie, giving another small wave to each person in the garage. "Hey, guys. Thanks for letting me be part of the band."

4    Mackenzie couldn't believe how shy she felt; but then again, she had never had to sing by herself before. She had sung in choruses for years, but she had never had a solo. Standing in a group and singing with everybody else was easy, but singing by herself was a whole different story.

5    Mackenzie and Cameron knew each other because they had been members of several of the same choruses since they were little. He knew she was a good singer, so he had invited her to be part of the band he was putting together. Cameron's best friend Tommy played the electric bass guitar, and a girl Mackenzie knew from school named Ashley stood behind a keyboard. The big surprise was seeing Grayson on the drums. He was a really quiet kid, and a lot of students at school thought he was kind of weird. He lifted his drumsticks and gave Mackenzie a little nod.

6    "What's the band's name?" asked Mackenzie. 7    "The Racket," replied Cameron. "What do you think?"

8    "Like a tennis racket?"

9    "No, my grandma was here the other day when we practiced, and she said, 'You sure make a racket out there, don't you?' So I thought that might be a good name, but the first thing you thought of was a tennis racket, so maybe not."

10    "We'll figure out the name later," Tommy insisted. "Right now, let's rock!" He began plucking up and down the strings of the bass, and a deep, steady run of notes blasted from the amplifiers that sat in the corners of the garage. Grayson picked up the rhythm and began pounding out a beat. Cameron handed Mackenzie a sheet with lyrics and yelled over the music, "Do you know this song?"

11    Mackenzie didn't recognize the title, so Cameron sang the lyrics the first two times the band played through it, and Mackenzie quickly picked up on the melody. The third time through, Mackenzie stood at the mike with the lyric sheet in hand and took over on lead vocals. She was concentrating so much on singing well, she completely forgot about her nerves, and when the song ended, the other band members yelled out, "Yeah! Great job!"

12    The Racket worked on three other songs, and before Mackenzie knew it, two hours had gone by and practice was over. While everyone started packing up their instruments, Cameron said, "We've got one month left until the show, so I think it's realistic to have three or four songs that we can play well enough for the performance."

13    "Performance?" Mackenzie asked. "What performance?"

14    "We're going to play at the school's Talent Days festival next month," Cameron explained.

15    And just like that, Mackenzie's stomach started doing flip-flops again.

As indicated, provide either a cause or an effect to complete each cause-and-effect relationship below. There may be more than one possible answer, but the cause or effect you provide must make sense according to events in story.

1. **cause:** _____

   **effect:** A loud *kerrrrang!* sound came from the garage.

2. **cause:** _____

   **effect:** Mackenzie's stomach started doing flip-fops again.

3. **cause:** Mackenzie did not recognize the title of the song the band was playing.

   **effect:** _____

4. **cause:** Cameron knew Mackenzie was a good singer.

   **effect:** _____

5. Provide your own example of a cause-and-effect relationship from the story.

   **cause:** _____

   **effect:** _____

6. What four instruments are played in the band?

   _____  _____  _____  _____

7. What inspired Cameron to name the band *The Racket*?

   _____

8. Mackenzie has been singing for years, so why is she nervous about singing with the band?

   _____

9. Why does Mackenzie stop feeling nervous during practice?

   _____

10. Why is Mackenzie surprised to discover that Grayson is in the band?

    _____

11. If you formed a band, what would you call it? Why?

    _____

    _____

    _____

# History of the Electric Guitar

*How did a mutant harp take over the world?*

1    A few thousand years ago, a favorite musical instrument in many cultures was the harp. It was a wooden frame that held strings of different lengths. The strings were plucked to make music, with each string giving off a different sound based on its thickness or length. Then, someone built a harp with strings that stretched partly over a hollow "sound" box, and partly over a solid board. The musician could press the strings against the board, and it had the same effect as shortening the string: it changed the sound. This meant the same range of notes could be played using just a few strings. This instrument was called a *psaltery*. A musician had more choices to create different notes. Later innovations gave birth to new designs and stringed instruments evolved: the lute, the mandolin, the dulcimer, the fiddle, and finally, about 80 years ago, the electric guitar.

2    The guitar of a few hundred years ago was small and quiet. It was played more often at home than in public. As the instrument became more popular, more music was written for it. Larger guitars were built. Experiments with metal strings helped make them play at a higher volume. Louder instruments were important in the large venues and concert halls that were becoming popular.

3    The solution to amplifying sound for large audiences and outdoor venues came in the 1930s. We don't know the specific person who invented the electric guitar. Many hobbyists tried on their own to come up with ways to amplify the sound coming from resonating, or vibrating, strings. The guitar was used in many kinds of popular music because it was portable, affordable, and could be practiced quietly and conveniently. In the 1930s, the rising stars of jazz, bluegrass, gospel, and blues all favored it. The birth of the electric guitar fit in well with the birth and rise of the music recording industry.

4    As electric guitars grew in popularity, some musicians became attached to their instruments. Many musicians named their guitars. In the 1940s, two men were fighting about a woman named Lucille. In their tussle, they set a building on fire. Blues star B. B. King's prized guitar was in the building. King ran into the burning building to save it and named his guitar "Lucille" from that day on.

5    The next decade saw the birth of the solid-body electric guitar, which is what most people recognize today. The most famous electric guitar is likely the Fender Stratocaster. This guitar was introduced in 1954. It was played by both Buddy Holly and John Lennon of the Beatles.

6    The electric guitar came to dominate popular music in the 1950s and 1960s. It was played by solo artists and in groups, and it was used for almost every style of music. In the 1960s, open air concerts, such as Woodstock, required huge volume and fancier effects. Many artists, such as Jimi Hendrix, chose the electric guitar as their mainstay instrument. Hendrix was left handed, so he flipped his right-handed guitars over and strung them in reverse.

7    Since the 1960s, the electric guitar has continued to develop in surprising ways. Many bluegrass, folk, and country bands use electric guitars similar to acoustic ones. They rely on electricity only for amplification. Rock and heavy metal bands often prefer solid-body guitars with controls for pitch, volume, tone, and reverberation. They often have a tremolo bar for effects as well. Some electric guitars even have two necks. One neck holds six strings, and the other neck holds twelve. Jimmy Page of Led Zeppelin played one these two-necked guitars in the classic song "Stairway to Heaven."

8    The next step in the electric guitar's evolution might be making "air guitar" a reality. New technologies are being developed so you can "play" the electric guitar with no guitar at all!

1. Which of the following types of music is LEAST likely to use an electric guitar? Place a checkmark on the line of the best answer.

_____ blues          _____ country

_____ jazz           _____ classical

2. Which of the following instruments was NOT mentioned in the text as being an ancestor of the guitar? Place a checkmark on the line of the correct answer.

_____ lyre           _____ harp

_____ lute           _____ fiddle

3. How does the author organize the text? Place a checkmark on the line of the best answer.

_____ comparing and contrasting          _____ cause and effect

_____ time order                         _____ subject

4. Who was "Lucille"?

_____

5. How were Jimi Hendrix's guitars different from most other guitars?

_____

_____

6. A guitar's neck forms the fingerboard. When a string is pressed against the fingerboard, it shortens the part of the string that will vibrate when it is plucked. Why is this important?

_____

_____

7. What was the main reason for inventing guitars that were electric?

_____

8. Do you play an instrument? If so, which instrument, and why did you choose it? If not, is there an instrument you would like to learn how to play? Why?

_____

_____

_____

_____

# It's . . . The Racket!

*Will Mackenzie's nerves get the better of her when she has to perform live?*

1    Mackenzie stood backstage and peeked around the curtain. She saw that every seat in the auditorium was filled, and people even stood along the back wall. She had never seen the place so crowded. It was the second night of her school's Talent Days festival, and the band she sang with—The Racket—was about to perform. She had gotten used to singing with the group, and she no longer felt at all nervous performing with them during practices, but the idea of standing out on the stage and singing to the crowd was making her head hurt.

2    They had spent the last month working hard to perfect a few songs for tonight's show, and at their final practice the day before, everybody felt really confident. They would play "Louie, Louie," "I Wanna Hold Your Hand," and an original song written by their drummer, Grayson, called "Let's Make a Racket!" They hoped to get the audience to shout along with the song's chorus, which was the same as the title. During Grayson's song, each band member would also get a chance to perform a short solo.

3    Mackenzie turned from where she had been watching the audience and saw her bandmates hopping around and high-fiving each other. She couldn't tell if they were just excited or trying to work out their nerves, but Mackenzie knew how she felt: terrified. An image kept running through her mind that she couldn't seem to turn off. She imagined walking onstage, opening her mouth to sing, but nothing would come out. As ridiculous as Mackenzie knew this scenario to be, a small, scared part of her couldn't stop thinking about it.

4    Onstage, a student finished reading a poem, and the audience applauded. When the girl came offstage, Principal Castillo said, "Great job, Emily." Then, the principal turned to Mackenzie and the others. "Are you guys ready?"

5    Principal Castillo strode onstage and announced, "Thank you, Emily, for that lovely poem. Next up, we have Mason Jr. High's first official rock band. Ladies and gentlemen, The Racket!"

6    As the band members headed out onstage, Mackenzie felt like she was on autopilot. Her legs moved and carried her over to the microphone, but her mind seemed to be hovering somewhere nearby. Adrenaline rushed through her body, and before she even knew it, the first song was halfway done. All of the practicing was paying off. Mackenzie knew the songs so well, she really didn't have to think much about what she was doing. It all came automatically, and she realized suddenly that she was enjoying the moment. She could hear the crowd cheering, but it was difficult to make out any specific faces because of the bright stage lights. So she just carried on like the audience wasn't really there, and it was no different than being at practice.

7    The highlight of the performance came during Grayson's song. As Mackenzie yelled out the chorus, the audience echoed back even louder: "Let's make a racket!" But then Grayson had his turn to perform a drum solo, and jaws dropped throughout the audience. The quietest kid in school turned out to a beast on the drums! Even the other members of The Racket were stunned by how well he played. At the end, the audience jumped to its feet and roared with appreciation. Grayson just gave a little nod and continued with the beat that would take the band to the end of the song.

8    As The Racket ran offstage, waving to the audience, Principal Castillo smiled at them and said, "I have a feeling I know who's going to take the prize for Audience Favorite this year."

9    Mackenzie wasn't too worried about the prize, though. She knew she had already gotten something even better: the confidence to perform.

**1.** Write a one-sentence summary of the story.

_____

**2.** Which of the following does NOT describe one of the story's themes? Place a checkmark on the line of the best answer.

_____ Trying new things, even if they make you nervous, can be rewarding.

_____ People often have unexpected talents.

_____ A bit of luck can lead to unexpected rewards.

_____ With hard work, you can achieve great things.

**3.** How was the song "Let's Make a Racket!" different from the other two songs the band played?

_____

**4.** Why do you think it helped Mackenzie's nervousness that she couldn't see the audience very well?

_____

**5.** Which of the following was NOT a song played by The Racket? Place a checkmark on the line of the correct answer.

_____ "Wild Thing"          _____ "Let's Make a Racket!"

_____ "Louie, Louie"          _____ "I Wanna Hold Your Hand"

**6.** Despite being scared, Mackenzie went onstage and preformed anyway. What does this tell you about her character?

_____

**7.** Why was Grayson's performance in particular a surprise to the audience?

_____

**8.** Why wasn't Mackenzie worried about whether or not the band would win a prize?

_____

**9.** Have you ever met someone who later surprised you by having a talent or an aspect of his or her personality that you didn't expect? Explain what it was that surprised you and why it was surprising.

_____

_____

_____

# Top Dog

*How did the Westminster Dog Show become so popular?*

1    The winner of a prestigious award embarks on a media tour in New York City. Along the way, she visits the Empire State Building, meets Donald Trump, and rings the bell to open the market at the New York Stock Exchange. These are special honors, and not just because they happened to an award winner—they happened to an award-winning *dog*!

2    In 2014, it was a fox terrier named Sadie that won Best in Show at the Westminster Dog Show, the highest award at this time-honored event. Dating back to 1877, the contest is second only to the Kentucky Derby—by just one year—for being the longest-running sporting event held in the United States. A group of sportsmen decided they wanted to showcase their dogs in one setting. They organized the first Westminster event, and received more than 1,200 entries.

3    The show was an immediate success. It attracted tens of thousands of spectators. In fact, the organizers extended the first event from a three-day show to four days based on its popularity. All proceeds from the extra day were donated to the ASPCA, the American Society for the Prevention of Cruelty to Animals.

4    By 1905, the Westminster Dog Show was the largest dog show in the world. Many famous people have taken part in the show during its history. Businessman J. P. Morgan brought his collies to the show in the 1890s. During the same time, journalist Nellie Bly showed her Maltese. Lou Gehrig, the famous New York Yankee, entered his German shepherd dog in the 1933 show.

5    Besides famous visitors, Westminster is also known for its support of important causes. During 1918–1919, the show's profits were donated to the American Red Cross to support efforts during World War I. During World War II, proceeds from the show were donated to the American Red Cross, Dogs for Defense, and the National War Fund. In more recent years, Westminster established an annual scholarship for students of veterinary medicine. In 2006, the show honored individuals and groups in the dog community that had contributed to rescue and recovery work following the Gulf Coast hurricanes of 2005.

6    Of course, the Westminster show is more than celebrity glamour and charity work. Dogs competing at the show must be champions that meet strict breed standards recognized by the American Kennel Club (AKC). A champion dog is one that has attended dog shows and earned a required number of points. During the show, a group of judges assesses each dog. They look for dogs that exhibit good temperament and overall good health.

7    Judges also examine each contestant to see how closely it meets the breed standard. These standards vary, depending on the breed. Anything from eye shape, fur markings, and nose color can be reviewed during judging. After the physical exam, judges observe each dog's gait as it walks or trots around the exhibition space. Judges get to see how all the breed standards display as the dog is in motion.

8    The modern Westminster show takes place over the course of two days. Tickets are in high demand, and often the show sells out each day. Those who aren't lucky enough to purchase their ticket in time can still enjoy the show. Unlike the early days of the contest, viewers can watch from the comforts of their home. The show is nationally televised, and, in 2005, Westminster began streaming video coverage of its event on the Westminster website.

**I.** Classify the following statements as **T** if a statement is true or **F** if a statement is false.

_____ The Westminster Dog Show is the longest-running sporting event the United States.

_____ All of the dogs competing in the Westminster Dog Show have already won honors in other dog shows.

_____ Dogs race through agility courses as one part of the Westminster Dog Show competition.

_____ A ticket to the show is the only way to view the competition.

_____ Throughout its 100+ years, many famous celebrities have attended the Westminster Dog Show.

_____ The way a dog looks is the only factor used to determine whether or not it will win top honors for its breed.

**2.** What does AKC stand for? Place a checkmark on the line of the correct answer.

_____ Associated Kennel Competition          _____ American Kennel Club

_____ American Kennel Canines          _____ Association of Kindness to Canines

**3.** On the line following each date, write a short sentence describing the important event from that year described in the text.

1877: _____

1905: _____

1918: _____

2006: _____

2014: _____

**4.** Does the author believe the Westminster Dog Show is good for dogs or not good for dogs? Support your answer with evidence from the text.

_____

_____

_____

_____

**5.** Describe your own pet(s), or a pet you would like to have.

_____

_____

# First-Class Dog

*How do people form bonds with their pets?*

1   Lorenzo inhaled deeply and looked to his parents for a bit of reassurance. Just from their smiles, he knew what they were thinking: *You'll do fine.*

2   Lorenzo slowly opened the metal door leading into the auditorium and peeked inside. His dog, Mia, waited until Lorenzo walked into the auditorium, and then she followed briskly behind him.

3   "Good girl, Mia!" Lorenzo praised her.

4   After researching breeds that were known for their loyalty and good nature, Lorenzo's family had adopted Mia from the local dog shelter during the past summer. Mia was a collie, and it was Lorenzo who discovered that collies are known for their intelligence and friendliness. He explained to his parents that this type of dog would match well with their family's lifestyle. Lorenzo's younger siblings were still very young, and their new dog would need to be gentle with children. Within a few weeks, they found and adopted Mia, a mixed breed dog that was mostly collie.

5   Like most dogs, Mia needed a basic obedience class to learn commands, so Lorenzo attended a class with her. The instructor had been impressed with their bond. He recommended that Lorenzo try agility with Mia, and now here they were, ready to begin the first class.

6   "Hello! You must be Lorenzo Martinez," a friendly woman said, approaching Lorenzo. "And this must be Mia."

7   "We're Lorenzo's parents, Margarita and Rodrigo," said Mrs. Martinez, extending her hand. The woman shook it, explaining that she was Melanie, the instructor.

8   "I watched some videos online before we came to class," said Lorenzo, "but I didn't realize how enormous a space we'd be in!"

9   Melanie nodded. "Yes, we offer advanced classes over there." She pointed to the left, where a small group of dogs and people were working together. One dog had just begun to run the agility course, and its owner ran alongside, guiding it. Melanie noticed the family had shifted their attention to this advanced class. "It's good that you're a little early; you can watch the advanced dogs run the entire course."

10   Melanie patted Mia's head. "For this first class, we'll have the handlers teach their dogs to focus on them. Lorenzo, it'll be your job to establish a strong bond with Mia. You will cue her every move on the course."

11   After watching another dog finish the advanced course, Lorenzo asked Melanie to describe each obstacle. "The A-frame," she began, "is the one with the two ramps that meet to form an 'A' shape. The dogwalk is the long, narrow obstacle. I like to think of it as a balance beam for dogs."

12   Lorenzo chuckled, "I don't think Mia's ready to become a stunt dog. I took her to a dog park at the city a few weeks ago, and I was able to get her to jump through the tire jump."

13   Melanie smiled and turned back toward the advanced class, pointing out each obstacle. "Just like at the park, the tire jump is a tire suspended from a frame. The bar jump is what people usually think of when they hear *agility*." Melanie gestured to a long bar with supports on either side. "The bar's height is adjusted based on the size of the dog jumping it. This is very similar to the jumps that are used in equestrian events."

14   "We attended an equestrian event last year," said Mrs. Martinez. "My cousin likes to ride horses, and I thought Lorenzo would enjoy watching it."

15   Lorenzo smiled. "I did—but I didn't think I'd be doing something similar with a dog someday!"

**1.** Who is the main character in the story? _____

**2.** What is the setting? _____

**3.** What breed of dog is Mia? _____

**4.** What are the characteristics of the breed, and why did Lorenzo think they would be a good match for the family?

_____

_____

**5.** Do you think Mia will succeed at agility? Support your answer with evidence from the text.

_____

_____

_____

_____

**6.** If a reader does not know the meaning of the word *equestrian,* what context clue does the author provide to help clarify the meaning?

_____

_____

_____

_____

**7.** Which of the following is NOT a piece of dog agility equipment described in the story? Place a checkmark on the line of the correct answer.

_____ A-frame ramp                _____ dogwalk

_____ suspended tire              _____ tunnel

**8.** Think of a human sports and physical competition. Which one do you think is the best comparison to dog agility? Write the sport you chose, and then explain your answer.

_____

_____

_____

_____

# Living a Dream

*What do you enjoy doing that might become a rewarding career?*

1    Cesar Millan always had a way with animals. Cesar lived on his grandfather's cattle ranch when he was very young, and the animals seemed to sense that Cesar was trustworthy. They followed him everywhere he went. When he was five, Cesar's family moved to Mazatlán, Mexico, where they had chickens, exotic birds, a pig, and dogs. Cesar spent much of his time training and bonding with the dogs. In spite of being bullied for his natural way with animals, Cesar persisted. At the age of 13, he realized that his dream was to become the best dog trainer in the world.

2    The United States represented an opportunity for Cesar to realize his dream. At the age of 21, he left his family behind and moved to California. When he arrived, Cesar did not speak a word of English, and he struggled during these early days, even living on the streets for the first few months after his arrival.

3    Cesar eventually found a job as a dog groomer. Soon after, he moved to a part of Los Angeles called *Inglewood*. Determined to fulfill his dream, he introduced himself to his new neighbors and offered them dog-walking services and free training—and many of their dogs needed intensive training. Cesar was ready for the challenge, and he soon won his neighbors' respect. He became known as the neighbor who rollerbladed down the street with as many as 12 dogs at his side!

4    After this success in his local neighborhood, Cesar opened a modest dog-training center. Many of his clients came from upscale areas, such as Beverly Hills. One of these clients, an actress named Jada Pinkett-Smith, believed in him. When Cesar explained to her that he wanted to be on television, Jada offered to assist him. She paid for a tutor so Cesar could become fluent in English.

5    During this time, Cesar was featured in an article in the *Los Angeles Times*. He told the interviewer about his desire to have a TV show, and the story caught the interest of several television producers. When they visited him, Cesar had each one meet his beloved pet pit bull, Daddy. Cesar trusted Daddy's instincts. He watched to see how Daddy reacted to each person.

6    The producers from one network passed Daddy's test. In 2004, Cesar's show, *The Dog Whisperer,* debuted. The show went on to become the top-rated show on its channel, and Cesar became a household name.

7    Cesar's dog-training method is unusual. While some dog trainers focus on the dog, Cesar focuses on the dog owner. His goal is to train the dog owner to be calm and assertive. When he was very young, Cesar learned from his grandfather that dogs experience the world using their senses, so this became the basis for Cesar's approach with dogs. He maintains eye contact with a dog, because looking directly into its eyes is like saying, "I am in charge."

8    Some dog owners bring their dogs to Cesar because their dogs are nervous. If he is working with a nervous dog, Cesar's response is to calmly ignore the dog's nervous behavior. This means no eye contact. Over time, the dog learns that this calm response means the person—Cesar—is in the dominant position. Eventually, the dog becomes calmer because it understands it should listen to the dominant person.

9    Cesar maintains a website, www.cesarsway.com. He uses it to share information about dog training, dog behavior, and dog rescue. He lives on a 43-acre ranch in Santa Clarita, California. Here, he also operates the Dog Psychology Center. Cesar realized his dream of becoming a dog trainer. One of his new goals is to turn a part of his ranch into a rescue for dogs that have been abused or neglected.

**1.** According to the text, what was Cesar Millan's dream? Place a checkmark on the line of the correct answer.

_____ to have his own TV show          _____ to be the best dog trainer in the world

_____ to train dogs in Hollywood          _____ to have his own website

**2.** Who was Daddy? Place a checkmark on the line of the correct answer.

_____ Cesar's grandfather          _____ Jada Pinkett-Smith's dog

_____ Cesar's pit bull          _____ the first dog Cesar trained

**3.** What was the name of Cesar Millan's TV show? _____

**4.** Is this text an autobiography or biography? Explain your answer.

_____

_____

_____

**5.** What actions did Cesar Millan take to work toward his success? Provide three examples.

_____

_____

**6.** Provide three examples of how others helped Cesar Millan achieve his success.

_____

_____

_____

**7.** How does the author organize the text? Place a checkmark on the line of the best answer.

_____ grouping similar ideas          _____ describing the steps of a process

_____ time order          _____ comparing and contrasting

**8.** The author describes how Cesar watched the way his dog reacted to each producer in order to decide which producer to choose. How do you think the dog reacted when he didn't like someone? How did the dog react when he did like someone?

_____

_____

_____

# Preparing for the Iditarod Trail

*What is the Iditarod, and how do contestants prepare for it?*

1   Jo Smith groans. It is September in Fairbanks, Alaska, and her father's alarm goes off at 4:00 in the morning. She knows that it is time once again to begin preparing for the Iditarod Trail Sled Dog Race. The race is held each March, and the family has had a few months to relax and recover from last year's race. Mr. Smith didn't win, but he did finish in nine days. Competing in the race is a family tradition. Both of her grandfathers led teams in the race, and her father first met her mother there.

2   A musher and a team of twelve to sixteen dogs begin the race in the city of Anchorage, Alaska. The start in Anchorage is more of a ceremony and an exhibition. The race starts again, officially, in the city of Willow. The musher and his or her team of dogs runs through often bitterly cold and snowy conditions until they finish the event in Nome, traveling over 1,000 miles. Jo is proud of her father for running in the event each year. She knows how unique her family's hobby is—only about 50 teams compete in the race, and there's no other race like it.

3   The race starts on the first Saturday in March, so the Smith family spends about eight months preparing. Her dad has to stay in top shape to race, and he begins each day with a ten-mile run. Jo's main job is to help take care of the sled dogs. In fact, the Smith family makes its living raising sled dogs. Jo is proud of her contribution to both the family's success in the race and in business. Although other breeds of dogs may compete in the event, the Smiths breed and raise Siberian Huskies.

4   The Smiths train at least twenty dogs each year to compete in the Iditarod, and the top sixteen of them will participate in the event. The dogs will have time to adjust to one another and compete well together as a team. It is part of Jo's job to make sure they are properly fed and watered each morning and night. During the day, while Jo is at school, her older brother and sister make sure the dogs get their proper meals and train them to run in the race.

5   The Smiths begin training the dogs for the race beginning in November. One of the rules of the race is that any dog that is injured or not physically fit needs to be removed from the team. The Smiths make sure that a veterinarian examines all of their dogs every two weeks during the training period to make sure that they stay in top condition and are fit to continue to train. The veterinarian also ensures that each dog has a small microchip. For most of the race, which sometimes is run through blizzard conditions, no spectators will be watching the competitors, so these microchips help race officials keep track of the dogs. Six of the dogs on a single team must still be running at the end of the race for a team to win.

7   The Smith family tries to stay in Nome until the race is over. Unlike many events, the Iditarod is not officially over until the last team crosses the finish line. A red lantern hangs at the finish line until the last team arrives. The Smiths hope that their team finishes in first next year so they can relax and cheer for all of the other teams as they arrive at the finish until, at last, the red lantern is extinguished.

**1.** In which state does the Iditarod take place? Place a checkmark on the line of the correct answer.

_____ Washington          _____ Montana

_____ North Dakota          _____ Alaska

**2.** Which of the following is a reasonable estimate for how long the Iditarod race lasts? Place a checkmark on the line of the best answer.

_____ 2 days          _____ 2 weeks

_____ 8 days          _____ 1 month

**3.** Describe how Jo helps her family prepare for the Iditarod.

_____

_____

**4.** Explain why the Iditarod starts twice.

_____

_____

**5.** Which of the following statements describes why the Smiths compete in the Iditarod each year? Place a checkmark on the line of the best answer.

_____ The winner of the Iditarod receives a large cash reward, and the Smiths hope that winning the money could change their lives.

_____ Racing in the Iditarod is a family tradition that has been passed down for a few generations.

_____ The Smiths raise sled dogs, and having their dogs race in the Iditarod means that the dogs will be worth a lot more money.

_____ Everyone who lives in their area is required to take part in the race as a form of emergency training in case of severe weather.

**6.** What is the significance of the red light at the race's finish line?

_____

**7.** Why does each dog have a microchip implanted under its skin?

_____

_____

**8.** What chores or other tasks do you do to help your family?

_____

# How About a Hybrid?

*Why might a hybrid car be a good investment?*

1  The Floyd family automobile is a clunker—it actually makes a rather loud clunking sound. Callum's dad knows his son is embarrassed to ride to school in it. Mr. Floyd asks both his wife and Callum to consider replacing their old vehicle with a newer model.

2  "I think it would be best to get a fuel-efficient car," says Callum as his mother nods in agreement. "I just did a report about cars in school. I think a hybrid car might be a wise investment. Hybrids use both electricity and gasoline as fuel sources."

3  "I've heard hybrids are a lot more expensive," says Mr. Floyd hesitantly.

4  "They're not as costly as many people think—and they are a lot quieter!" Callum chuckles. "We wouldn't have to turn up our music so loud to cover the engine noise."

5  "You have a good point there, Callum," his mother says. "We'll have to find the overall cost of operation. I know that the initial cost of the car might be more expensive, but because hybrid cars run on electricity, fuel is cheaper when gas prices increase."

6  Callum chimes in, "We would definitely save money on the cost of fuel in June, July, and August. It's almost summertime and gas prices are substantially higher in this area during the vacation season."

7  Mr. Floyd nods his head and ponders their information. "What if the car runs low on electricity while we're driving?"

8  "Public charging stations are more widely available now than ever before," notes Callum. "In addition, in an emergency you can rely on a switch over to gasoline power. You wouldn't want to do this too often, though, because then fuel becomes more expensive and you increase the amount of pollution you add to the environment."

9  Callum's mom adds, "That's an important thing for us to think about, too. Hybrid cars leave half of the carbon footprint of regular gasoline-powered vehicles. That means they add only half as much carbon to our atmosphere.

10  "We spend a lot of time sitting in traffic in the mornings, so that is definitely an important consideration, because we use a lot of fuel then," says Mr. Floyd. "Our emissions are tested in this area, too, and unfortunately I don't think our favorite clunker is going to pass its next test. I've seen it spew out black smoke while I've been idling and waiting for a red light to change."

11  Mrs. Floyd declares, "We certainly need to replace our car, then, and I understand that hybrid vehicles aren't even subjected to the emissions test in this area. That's a bonus!"

12  "Another factor we should think about is the speed at which we usually drive. Because hybrids are most efficient at lower speeds, it might be the optimal solution for us. This is the automobile we'd use for short-distance trips and non-freeway driving, so we'd primarily be using electricity for fuel. Gasoline is used mostly at higher speeds," Callum elaborates.

13  "Let's figure out the overall cost of driving a few hybrids and a few gasoline-powered cars, and then we can go take any candidates for purchase out for a test drive to decide what we like best," declares Mr. Floyd. "Callum, you can drive, too, because you just got your permit. I think someone who is so carefully helping us consider this choice should get an opportunity to decide what we'll purchase in the end."

14  "We haven't talked about the most important decision, though," says Mrs. Floyd.

15  "What color should we get?" asks Callum, and everyone laughs.

**I.** Write a sentence that summarizes the story.

_____

_____

**2.** What is the author's main purpose for writing the story? Place a checkmark on the line of the best answer.

_____ to tell an entertaining story about a family who needs to replace their old car

_____ to describe the benefits of owning a hybrid automobile

_____ to describe problems associated with owning a hybrid automobile

_____ to describe the inconvenience of auto emissions tests

**3.** What makes a hybrid automobile different from traditional automobiles?

_____

_____

**4.** Write a sentence describing the author's point of view about hybrid automobiles.

_____

**5.** Does the author support his or her point of view with sufficient evidence and sound reasoning? Cite examples from the text in your answer.

_____

_____

_____

_____

_____

**6.** If this story took place 50 years ago, how would it be different? What elements might be the same?

_____

_____

_____

**7.** Hybrid automobiles are one way to use fewer fossil fuels and reduce pollution. Name two others.

_____          _____

# The World Solar Challenge

*What are some of the requirements for the cars competing in the World Solar Challenge?*

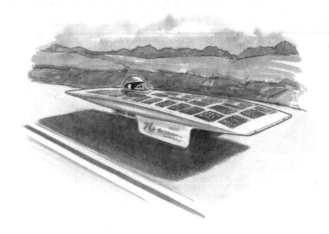

1    The World Solar Challenge (WSC) is a solar-powered vehicle race. This race lasts eight days and is now held every other year. The cars in the race travel south from Darwin to Adelaide, Australia. Each competing team covers over 3,000 kilometers. There are several solar car races, but the WSC is arguably the most famous. Teams from all around the world design and build vehicles for the competition. In 2013, 40 teams from 23 countries participated in the race. Hans Tholstrup organized the first three races. This Danish solar pioneer then sold the race to South Australia for its fifth running.

2    Teams that compete in the WSC represent many different colleges, companies, and research institutions. An American car company, General Motors, won the first event in 1987. A team sponsored by The Massachusetts Institute of Technology is the only other American team to win. The Delft University of Technology, from the city of Delft in the Netherlands, has sponsored the most winners.

3    Each team in the event enters a car that adheres to the specifications of its class of entry. In 2013, these classes included the Challenger, Cruiser, and Adventure classes. In the Challenger class, each team completes the WSC in one single stage. Other specifications for each class include the number of drivers and wheels the car may have. The physical design of each car is determined by each team competing in the race. While the physical appearances of the cars differ, each car's roof has a large, flat surface covered with thin solar panels. These panels may cover no more than six square meters. All solar-powered cars competing in the WSC are built from extremely lightweight materials. These lightweight cars require less energy to move forward. Each car weighs about as much as a refrigerator.

4    The cars competing in the WSC can go up to speeds of 150 kilometers per hour (kp/h). The average speed in the 2013 race ranged from 75 kp/h in the Cruiser class to around 91 kp/h in the Challenger class. The cars are only allowed to store a maximum of five kilowatt hours of energy. The cars' designers use the principle of kinetic energy, or the energy of motion, to help generate additional energy while the vehicles are moving. All other energy the cars use must come from the sun. Unlike many races, the competing teams are generally friendly with one another. All participants in the race have to face the same obstacles.

5    In all classes, the competing teams must rely only on themselves and their own ingenuity to complete the race. The solar-powered cars in the WSC run on public roads. The race is held between eight o'clock in the morning and five o'clock at night. During the race there are mandatory checkpoints where observers of the cars are changed and team managers are updated. Teams can only perform basic maintenance at these checkpoints. For example, they can clean debris from the car or add air to the tires. If a major repair is required, such as battery replacement, the team is given a time penalty.

6    Race completion times in the 2013 WSC ranged between 33 and 41 hours. Two of the three winning teams were from the Netherlands. Teams from the Netherlands and Japan have most frequently won WSC events. The World Solar Challenge ultimately helps research teams develop more efficient solar-powered cars. The team that wins celebrates by dunking themselves in the fountain in Victoria Square in Adelaide.

**1.** Write a sentence to summarize each paragraph of the text.

    1. _____

    2. _____

    3. _____

    4. _____

    5. _____

**2.** Participants from which of the following nations have had the most success at the World Solar Challenge? Place a checkmark on the line of the best answer.

    _____ the United States         _____ China

    _____ the Netherlands         _____ Australia

**3.** List two of the requirements that vehicles must meet in order to compete in the World Solar Challenge.

    _____

    _____

**4.** Why do you think the speeds and distances in the text are described in terms of kilometers rather than miles?

    _____

    _____

**5.** Complete the sentence below.

    Each vehicle in the World Solar Challenge weighs about as much as _____ .

**6.** What do the winners of the WSC usually do as part of the celebration?

    _____

**7.** Other than entertainment, what do you think is a benefit that comes from having a race like the World Solar Challenge?

    _____

    _____

**8.** Imagine if all of the vehicles where you live were solar-powered. Describe how your town or city would be different than it is now with mostly gas-powered vehicles.

    _____

    _____

# Galaxie Guys

*What will Sebastian and Mr. Tucker find when they visit an auto salvage lot?*

1   Mr. Tucker drummed his hands on the steering wheel, keeping time with the beat. As usual, Sebastian's dad was blaring an old rock song on the radio. An announcer cut in: "That was The Zombies with 'She's Not There' on Oldies 104.8!"

2   "My turn!" Sebastian shouted. He leaned toward the radio buttons and pressed number 8. The sounds of violins and cellos filled the car as a string quartet replaced the enthusiastic voice of the deejay.

3   Mr. Tucker stopped drumming and began waving his hand through the air like a conductor. He smiled at his son and said, "You know, I don't mind switching back and forth after each song, but it's not entirely a fair trade. My songs last only about three minutes. Your songs go on for*ever*." They both laughed.

4   As they exited the freeway, Sebastian saw that they had arrived in an industrial part of town. Huge warehouses lined one side of the road, and the other side was a combination of large, empty concrete expanses and an occasional abandoned factory. Soon, they began passing a long, rusty metal fence that ran for at least two blocks into the distance. It was solid, so Sebastian could not see what was on the other side.

5   "We're here," Mr. Tucker announced, as he pointed ahead to a break in the fence, where a driveway led through to the other side. A huge sign above the driveway said *Morris's Auto Salvage.*

6   Mr. Tucker and Sebastian had been restoring a 1965 Ford Galaxie. Sebastian was mostly the assistant, handing his father tools and holding the shop light at just the right angle, but once in a while Mr. Tucker had Sebastian do some real work, like tightening bolts or cleaning the grease and oil off of parts. Today, they hoped to find a grille for the Galaxie at the salvage lot.

7   After they parked, Mr. Tucker went inside the office and spoke with the lot attendant. Sebastian waited outside and observed the rows of beat up old cars stretching away in all directions. Sebastian thought about new cars at a dealership and how they looked so clean and uniform, all the same models lined up in rows. The cars at the salvage lot could not have been more different. They were grouped somewhat by make and model, but beyond that, each car was entirely unique. One might be rusty, another missing its wheels and a trunk, and the next car might have some shine left, but the windshield was smashed. Sebastian loved the variety.

8   Mr. Tucker came out of the office and said, "I've got a map of the lot. We need to head down to the end of this row, turn left, and walk up three more rows. Then, we should spot some Galaxies."

9   By the time they reached the end of the first row, Sebastian had counted almost 100 cars. Quickly calculating in his head, he figured there had to be at least a couple thousand cars in the lot.

10   When they reached the section with Galaxies, there were three 1965 models similar to theirs. One still had a nice-looking grille on its front, so Mr. Tucker set down his toolkit, and they went to work. An hour later, they had the grille off. They lugged it back to the office.

11   After Mr. Tucker paid the attendant, he and Sebastian loaded the grille into the back of their car and headed for home.

12   "That place was really cool," Sebastian said as they drove off the lot. "Thanks for bringing me along." He flipped on the radio, and immediately punched button number 3. Old-timey country music came on, with a fiddle sawing away behind the twangy vocals of a singer from long ago. Mr. Tucker turned and gave Sebastian a surprised look. "I know, it's not classical, but I thought some variety would be more fun. Besides, I think these songs will be a lot shorter."

**1.** Why is the story titled *Galaxie Guys*?

_____

**2.** Why are Sebastian and his dad going to an auto salvage lot?

_____

**3.** Authors include sensory details to make their stories more interesting. Sensory details describe sights, sounds, smells, tastes, and textures experienced by the characters. Which two senses does the author provide details for in the story? Provide two examples for each sense.

Sense: _____

Example 1: _____

Example 2: _____

Sense: _____

Example 1: _____

Example 2: _____

**4.** Did Sebastian enjoy the trip to the auto salvage yard? How do you know?

_____

_____

**5.** What kind of relationship does Sebastian have with his dad? Support your answer with evidence from the text.

_____

_____

_____

**6.** Sebastian usually plays classical music in the car when it's his turn to choose. What do your think influenced his choice of a bluegrass station at the end of the story?

_____

_____

_____

**7.** When you get to choose music to play in the car, what do you choose? Why?

_____

_____

# Internment During WWII

*What could lead the United States government to lock up 100,000 innocent American citizens?*

1   President Franklin D. Roosevelt declared it "a date which will live in infamy." On December 7, 1941, with no warning, the Empire of Japan attacked the United States at Pearl Harbor in Hawaii. Until then, Americans had been reluctant to get involved in the two major conflicts happening at that time in the world. Europe was under siege by German forces. Nations in the western Pacific Ocean were being attacked by Japan. Americans saw these as foreign wars that the United States should not be involved in. Pearl Harbor changed that view overnight. Suddenly, the American military and citizens were mobilizing to join the efforts to defeat both Germany and Japan. The challenges of life during wartime would affect all Americans, but some Americans would be affected in an entirely unexpected way.

2   Soon after the attack, a wave of anti-Japanese feeling swept the country. Japan was now an official enemy of the United States. Fear and paranoia led many Americans to see anyone of Japanese descent as an enemy, too. Even Japanese-American citizens were viewed suspiciously as potential spies. Of course, all Americans did not feel this way, but anger about Pearl Harbor led many people to act in ways they might later regret.

3   Two months after the attack on Pearl Harbor, President Roosevelt signed a special order. It allowed the American military to create "exclusion zones" in the United States. Within these zones, the military had the right to exclude, or remove, anyone they felt might be a threat to American security. Most of the Pacific Coast was designated as an exclusion zone. The main target for exclusion in this zone was people of Japanese ancestry. Starting in March 1942, the military began ordering Japanese people in California, Oregon, and Washington to pack up and move to special camps where they could be monitored. More than 100,000 people were affected. Most of them were Japanese-American citizens, and many of their families had lived in the United States for decades.

4   With only a few days notice, the men, women, and children had to pack up a few belongings and report to processing centers.

Many business owners and farmers were forced to sell their shops or land with no time to get a fair price. Homes would sit empty and unprotected for however long the families would have to be detained. People's lives were not simply disrupted; many of them were devastated by the event.

5   After processing, families were put aboard trains that carried them to temporary assembly centers. From there, they would be assigned to long-term relocation centers. The relocation centers were usually made up of dozens, or even hundreds, of wooden army barracks. These buildings had no plumbing or kitchens. Armed guards surrounded the camps to ensure no one could leave.

6   Even though the people in the camps were locked in and living in primitive conditions, they still managed to make life bearable. Residents set about decorating their barracks as best they could, making the places seem more like homes. Outside, they planted whatever kinds of flowers or plants they could find. To a limited extent, life in the camp became similar to living in a small village. There were newspapers, barbershops, and baseballs teams. Still, they lacked what all Americans take for granted: freedom.

7   At the end of 1944, the Supreme Court finally ruled that detaining citizens—no matter what their ancestry—without just cause was illegal. Those detained were released, and the camps were closed. However, many people returned home to find their properties vandalized, robbed, or even taken over by others. Their lives would need to begin again from scratch.

8   Although it took another 40 years, the United States government officially apologized in 1988 for its actions against Japanese Americans during World War II. It was the final chapter in an event that lives in infamy.

**1.** List three main ideas presented in the text.

_____

_____

_____

**2.** Choose one of the ideas you wrote above, and identify details or evidence from the text that support the idea.

_____

_____

_____

**3.** Why were detained Japanese Americans finally allowed to return home? Place a checkmark on the line of the correct answer.

_____ The United States defeated Japan, and World War II ended.

_____ President Roosevelt declared the camps unjust, and he ordered the release of all detainees.

_____ The Supreme Court ruled that it was against the law to detain American citizens without just cause.

_____ The American people insisted that the camps were unjust, so their representatives in the U.S. Congress voted to close the camps and release the detainees.

**4.** Analyze the way *infamy* is used in the first and final sentences of the text. Which of the following best describes the meaning of *infamy*? Place a checkmark on the line of the best answer.

_____ an event that is unjust        _____ remembered for a long time

_____ a negative kind of fame        _____ a violent act during wartime

**5.** What did the detainees do to make life more bearable in the camps? Why do think these actions were important?

_____

_____

_____

_____

_____

# Into the Unknown

*How would it feel to be forced from your home and sent away?*

1    Araki sat at his desk, surveying the bedroom he might never see again. Down the hall in the living room, he could hear his parents arguing quietly. Mrs. Yamamoto insisted that they should try to run away to the east coast. She had family in Virginia, and if they could get across the country, maybe they could avoid detention. Mr. Yamamoto thought it was a bad idea. He had heard rumors that anyone who did not appear voluntarily for relocation would be sent to a special camp—a camp that was more like prison. He tried to calm his wife's anger and fear, insisting that it would be safest to simply do as they were instructed. Mr. Yamamoto was convinced that they would be gone at most a few months.

2    Five days earlier, the announcement had come that all people of Japanese descent—whether American citizens or not—would need to report to the processing center that had been hastily erected near the train station. The Yamamotos had seen the news reports; they knew what came next. They would be sent to one of the detention camps set up to hold Japanese Americans while America was at war with Japan. After the attack on Pearl Harbor, the American military had decided to take no chances: all people of Japanese ancestry were under suspicion of working for the enemy, especially those living on the west coast.

3    At first, the Yamamotos had assumed the order would not apply to them. They were American citizens. Their family had lived in the United States since the late-1800s. Besides, Araki's cousin served in the Army. How could they be spies? But it did not matter. They had to leave just like many of the other families in the neighborhood.

4    Mr. Yamamoto had spent the week closing up his flower shop. He had sold all of his live plants and fresh flowers to his main competitor, Mr. Hawkins. Mr. Hawkins refused to pay a fair price, though, because he knew Mr. Yamamoto had no choice but to take whatever he could get. When his dad came home from locking up the empty store, Araki could see the sadness and worry in his eyes.

5    The arguing in the living room had stopped, so Araki left his room and went to be with his parents. As he entered the room, he saw his mother had been crying. Araki sat next to his mom, and she reached out and took his hand. The three of them sat there silently, because there wasn't much else to be said. Several suitcases were stacked by the front door, ready for the family's early morning departure.

6    Shortly after sunrise the next morning, the family left. Araki and his mother stood on the sidewalk as Mr. Yamamoto locked the door, and then he joined them. They gave their home one last, fond look before heading down the block, a bag held in each of their six hands.

7    Araki wished it were a much farther walk, but the processing center at the train station was only ten minutes away. As they neared the station, he saw the line. Dozens of families stood outside the temporary building, waiting quietly for their turn. He recognized a few classmates from school, standing with their parents and siblings. Araki noticed that everyone was dressed nicely, including his family, and it was like they were all headed to a special event. In a strange way, they were.

8    Beyond the building, Araki saw a family that had completed their processing and now headed toward the train that would take them all away. Araki was surprised to feel a small bit of excitement. He had ridden on a train only once before, and he had loved it. The excitement mingled with the fear and anxiety he also felt. He hoped, somehow, the experience could be an adventure as much as an inconvenience. Only time would tell.

**I.** Who is the protagonist, or main character, in the story?

_____

**2.** The antagonist of a story is the opponent or enemy that the protagonist must struggle against. Identify the antagonist in this story.

_____

**3.** Do you think Araki defeats the antagonist? Why or why not? Cite evidence from the story in your answer.

_____

_____

_____

**4.** Why does Mr. Yamamoto think running away is a bad idea?

_____

**5.** Read or review the previous story, *Internment During WWII*. It is a nonfiction historical text about the same event affecting the fictional Yamamotos in this story. Compare and contrast the two texts. Which do you think is a more effective way to tell about history? Explain your answer.

_____

_____

_____

_____

_____

_____

_____

**6.** Based on what you have read in this story and the previous nonfiction text, make a prediction about Araki's experiences at the relocation camp. Support your prediction with evidence from the texts.

_____

_____

_____

_____

# The Good with the Bad

*Can something positive come from even the worst circumstances?*

1   The clock ticking on the mantle was the only sound in the living room, as Lila stared silently at the photographs in front of her. They showed her grandpa as a boy, standing with his family in front of a wooden army barracks. Lila took a deep breath and said, "I had no idea you had gone to one of those camps."

2   Lila was writing about her family's history for a school assignment, and when she began her research, she soon realized just how little she knew about her grandparents' lives from before she was born. She called Grandpa Araki right away and asked if she could come visit sometime and talk with him and Grandma Mai. Lila wanted to include interesting details from their childhoods in her report, but she especially wanted to know how they had met. What she had not expected was to learn that her grandparents had been relocated to an internment camp during World War II, like so many other Japanese Americans had been.

3   "Yes, our families had to go, too," Grandpa Araki explained. "We were living in Seattle, where my great-grandfather had settled in the 1800s, when Pearl Harbor was attacked. My father owned a flower shop there, and we lived in a neighborhood with many other Japanese Americans. A few months after the attack, we all received notice that our families must report for processing and detention, and next thing I knew, we were on a train headed to California."

4   "That's so unfair!" Lila exclaimed. "You were citizens, right? Did they think you were spies or something? Wow, being rounded up like that must have been really scary, and it sure doesn't sound like something that would happen in America."

5   "People across the country were scared, Lila," Grandpa Araki continued, "and most of those detained understood that fear was behind the detentions. Many people were angry about being moved, of course, but mostly everyone was resigned to the fact that they had to go. I was young, so mostly it was just confusing to me. I had to leave my school and the only house I had ever known, and instead I spent the next couple of years at the detention camp."

6   "How bad was it there?" Lila asked. "We've learned about the Holocaust in school, but I know it wasn't anything like that. Was it like a work camp, though?"

7   "People did work, but no one was forced to. The camp was surrounded by large fields, and many of the people farmed the land. The camp was a lot like a little village. There was a barbershop, a newsstand, a small grocery store, and even a school. Life goes on, even in an unfortunate circumstance such as being detained in the camp. After a while, we adjusted as best we could, and I made new friends, went to school, and had fun. Believe it or not, that's where I first started playing baseball. Our camp had several teams, and we played as often as we could. There were also dances almost every week."

8   "Still, you couldn't leave the camp," Lila pointed out. "You were basically in jail!"

9   "It was a big mistake made by those in power," Grandpa Araki agrees. "But, you know, I've never lost faith in America, because even after making a mistake as big as the detention camps were, the government was already working to right the wrong. Even before the war ended, the Supreme Court declared the camps unjust, and we were on our way home."

10   So far, Grandma Mai had been quiet, but now she had something to say. "Lila, the camps were not a good thing, but there was one important and very positive outcome that would not have happened without the camps."

11   "What's that, Grandma?"

12   "The detention camp is where your grandpa and I met!"

**1.** Write a few sentences summarizing the story.

_____

_____

_____

**2.** Why does Grandpa Araki say the camp was "like a little village"?

_____

**3.** How would the story be different if Grandpa Araki had spent his life angry and bitter about his experiences at the camp?

_____

_____

**4.** Why does Grandpa Araki say he "never lost faith in America," despite his family's unjust detention?

_____

_____

**5.** Which of the following best describes Lila's reason for visiting her grandparents? Place a checkmark on the line of the best answer.

_____ When Lila found out that her grandparents had lived at one of the relocation camps, she wanted to learn more about their experiences.

_____ As part of a school assignment, Lila wanted to interview her grandparents about their lives.

_____ Lila was writing a school report about the relocation camps, and she wanted to get a first-hand account of her grandparents' experiences.

_____ Lila was at her grandparents' house for a holiday visit.

**6.** What were two positive events for her grandparents that occurred at the camp?

_____

_____

**7.** Have you ever had something positive happen as a result of an otherwise negative event? Describe what happened, or describe an imaginary scenario in which a negative event has some kind of positive aspect to it.

_____

_____

# Discover Your Family Tree

*How can the Internet help us learn more about our past?*

1   What is your *genealogy*? In other words, what is the history of your family, your ancestors, and how are you all related? Many people are curious and want to learn more about their genealogy. In fact, tracing ancestries and family trees is a fairly big business, especially since the Internet has made it much easier to dig into those family forests. In the past, those who wanted to know more about their ancestors had to rely on written records, but those records were not always easily accessible or accurate. They also looked through old military records and sifted through love letters and other correspondences found in attic trunks. But nothing was as priceless or enjoyable as listening to the stories told by grandparents, great-grandparents, and aunts and uncles. Today, however, if what you are looking for is a traceable record of your family and ancestry, the Internet can be an invaluable source.

2   With genealogy, it helps to think like a detective. Good detectives always do their homework, which is, in this case, research. Start by looking for free online sites that can help guide you. You won't find all of the information you need in one place, so expect to do some digging. But believe it or not, hard work is part of the fun—and it can take you to unexpected places. Leave yourself open to new discoveries and the places they take you. You will learn a lot about your family on the journey.

3   After you have talked with your closest living relatives and documented your findings, it's time to start your Internet search. Good detectives take good notes, so keep track of all of your searches as you proceed. You don't want to waste time looking up information more than once, simply because you forgot to write down an important name or birth date.

4   A good place to start on the Internet is with obituary and cemetery databases. You can look at large online archives, but even better is to search the records of local newspapers. You may not end up with solid facts about your family's history, but most likely they will provide clues to your family puzzle. Your next step may be looking at online census records. The farther back you go in time, the more challenging your search may become. Census records are not always accurate. Names are sometimes misspelled, and there may be gaps in the records. Again, just keep recording your clues and collecting the pieces of your puzzle.

5   Once you have pinpointed where your family members may have lived, you can visit location specific websites, such as local libraries and public records databases. These databases allow you to search newspaper articles, biographies, and public histories. You can often focus your searches by category, such as occupation, military service, schools, churches, or social organizations.

6   At some point, your search will broaden. You can look online for other people searching the same surnames and locations to see if they can help you. Be sure to document and check your facts as you go. Don't get discouraged if you follow the wrong path for awhile. That can happen. Simply back up to a point in time where you know the facts are right, and then start again.

7   Eventually, you may decide to use one of the many online family tree search sites. These sites may give you access to a wide variety of documents you would be unable to find on your own. Some of the sites offer free trials to get you started, and then you pay a fee if you wish to continue. Do a little research beforehand to be sure you choose a reliable site.

8   As the branches of your tree grow, the search will grow as well. But the challenge of the search for your family roots is also what makes it rewarding and so much fun.

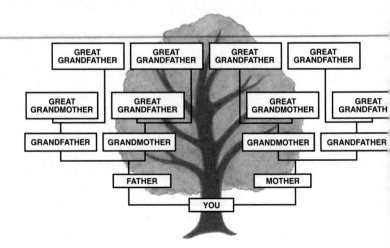

**1.** How is the text organized? Place a checkmark on the line of the best answer.

_____ time order                     _____ steps of a process

_____ comparing and contrasting      _____ similar ideas

**2.** What is *genealogy*?

_____

**3.** What occupation does the author compare someone studying genealogy to?

_____

**4.** Which of the following best summarizes the author's point of view about genealogical research? Place a checkmark on the line of the best answer.

_____ Researching your family's genealogy can be a lot of work, but the work is rewarding.

_____ The easiest way to research your family's genealogy is to use an Internet family tree search service.

_____ Public record databases contain many errors and gaps in information, so they should mostly be avoided.

_____ You must take notes when you are researching your family's genealogy, otherwise you will have to work twice as hard.

**5.** What is the author's advice if you follow a path back through your family's history, but the path turns out to be wrong?

_____

_____

**6.** List three places mentioned in the text where someone can look for information about their family's history.

_____   _____   _____

**7.** According to the text, what is the first step you should take if you want information about your family's history?

_____

**8.** Write a short paragraph describing what you know about your family's history, such as where your ancestors lived, what your grandparents did for a living, and so on.

_____

_____

# A Beautiful Day for Bluegrass

*What does Charley experience at his first bluegrass festival?*

1    As Charley followed his parents through the crowd, he hung back several feet to appear as if he were there by himself. In one hand, he held a paper plate with a half eaten funnel cake on it, and he walked slowly so he wouldn't bump into someone and drop it. With his other hand, he was tearing off big doughy, sugary bites and sticking them in his mouth. Charley ate funnel cake only a couple of times a year, whenever they went to a fair or festival, so he was savoring each sweet, chewy bite.

2    Charley and his parents had driven forty-five minutes outside of the city to attend the Watkins Valley Bluegrass Festival. After parking with what had seemed like a thousand other cars in a gigantic empty field, they had walked for several minutes to reach the front entrance to the festival. Inside the main grounds, Charley couldn't believe how many people had come out to listen to the music. He had never been in such a crowded place before.

3    Right away, Charley and his parents had rushed to the main stage. Buck Wilson and the Mountain Valley Boys were performing, and they were favorites of Charley's dad. His dad was a big fan of bluegrass, but to Charley, all the songs sounded kind of the same. A huge area in front of the stage was crammed with people spread out on blankets or sitting on the weedy ground. Families had picnic baskets and coolers with them, and here and there people were dancing to the upbeat fiddle music played onstage. Huge speakers on either side of the stage amplified the instruments and carried the tunes to the far reaches of the festival grounds. They had managed to find a spot to stand toward the back of the crowd. Charley was caught up in the cheerfulness of the event, and he had to admit, the old-timey music was hard not to like.

4    The market area where they strolled now was lined with booths selling all sorts of traditional craft items. He saw a woman weaving baskets. A man sold hand-carved wooden bowls. Lots of vendors sold instruments, like harmonicas or fiddles. Outside one booth, a man with a long, white beard sat on a stool playing a banjo. Next to him was an elderly man keeping the beat with a pair of spoons. He held the spoons

back-to-back in one hand, and then slapped them against his thigh, the palm of his other hand, and ran them up and down his arm. Charley couldn't stop smiling; it was such a great sound and a fun way to make music. The man grinned right back at Charley. When the song ended, the crowd that had gathered around them burst into cheers.

5    Charley's dad tapped him on the shoulder and signaled that they needed to head back toward the main stage. His dad's brother, Uncle Vernon, was in the band scheduled to play next. As they left the market area, they walked past all the food vendors. The odors of corn dogs, hamburgers, BBQ ribs, French fries, and a dozen other foods all mingled together into a slightly sweet, meaty smell that was familiar from almost every fair Charley had ever been to.

6    Charley and his parents found a spot to sit not too far from the front of the stage. Soon, Uncle Vernon and his band came out, and the audience politely clapped. Uncle Vernon held what looked like a really little guitar, but with a round body. When Charley asked his mom what it was, she told him it was a *mandolin*. Then, one of the other band members plugged in an electric guitar. Charley thought bluegrass players used only acoustic instruments. Soon, Uncle Vernon's band was ripping into a rocking bluegrass song, and Charley had to admit: it certainly did not sound like all the other bluegrass he had heard!

**1.** What is the main idea of this story? How does the author develop this idea? Cite evidence from the story in your answer.

_____

_____

_____

**2.** Why do you think Charley wants to pretend he is at the festival by himself?

_____

**3.** Which of the following instruments is NOT mentioned at some point in the story? Place a checkmark on the line of the correct answer.

_____ harmonica                _____ ukulele

_____ banjo                     _____ mandolin

**4.** Authors include sensory details to make their stories more interesting. Sensory details describe sights, sounds, smells, tastes, and textures experienced by the characters. Find examples in the text of details describing three different senses. Record the senses and examples below.

Sense: _____     Example: _____

Sense: _____     Example: _____

Sense: _____     Example: _____

**5.** How do Charley's feelings about bluegrass music change by the end of the story? Why do they change?

_____

_____

**6.** How would this story be different if it were told from Uncle Vernon's perspective? Give at least two examples.

_____

_____

_____

**7.** Compare and contrast the festival in the story to a fair, festival, or other event you have attended. Describe at least two ways they are similar and two ways they are different.

_____

_____

# Carrie Underwood

*After giving up on her dream, how did Carrie Underwood make it come true?*

1 Throughout the fourth season of *American Idol*, audiences watched—and cheered for—a young singer named Carrie Underwood. Her fans, known as "Carrie's Care Bears," loyally voted for her week after week so she would remain on the show. During the final episode in which the singers performed for votes, judge Simon Cowell predicted that Underwood would easily win the competition. He made another prediction, too: she would go on to be a hit-making superstar.

2 Cowell knew very well what he was talking about. At the finale a few days later, Carrie Underwood was crowned the champion of Season Four. Just a month later, she had the number one hit song in America, "Inside Your Heaven." It was quite a ride for a farm girl from a small town.

3 Carrie Underwood was born in 1983. She grew up on a farm near the small, rural town of Checotah, Oklahoma. From an early age, she loved singing, and she performed in talent shows and for the members of her church. As she got older, she also sang at local events, such as Checotah's annual Old Settler's Day Festival. She began to make a name for herself around town as a talented singer, and at least one local fan wanted to help her reach a wider audience. This admirer helped Underwood get an audition with Capitol Records in Nashville, Tennessee, the capital of country music.

4 She was only 14, but she impressed the people at Capitol. They planned to have her record a song for release as a single. Unfortunately, before they had a chance to finalize the agreement, changes occurred within the company. In the end, the contract was never written. Underwood went home empty-handed. Looking back, Underwood believes it was actually the best outcome. She has said that if she had begun her music career at such a young age, she would not have achieved the success she has now.

5 After the disappointment of Nashville, Underwood decided to give up on her dream of singing. Besides, she had other talents. In high school, she played basketball and softball, but she also excelled in academics. When Underwood graduated from high school in 2001, she had the second-highest grades in her class. A few months later, she headed off to college. She was ready to earn a degree and pursue life working at something other than singing.

6 But during the summer of 2004, Underwood decided to give her dream one more chance. The popular *American Idol* television show was holding auditions in St. Louis, Missouri. It was just a few hours drive away from where she lived in Oklahoma. Her successful audition that day changed her life forever.

7 As part of her *American Idol* win, Underwood earned a million-dollar recording contract. Right away, she headed into the studio, and she soon had not only her first number-one single, but she had an entire album ready for release as well. In the fall of 2005, her debut LP *Some Hearts* was released to immediate—and long-lasting—success. It went on to become the best-selling album of 2006. It was also the best-selling country album for the next *two* years.

8 Carrie Underwood's superstardom continued. Each of her next three albums rocketed to the top of both the country and pop music charts. Her singles routinely sell millions of copies to fans around the world. Underwood has also won dozens of honors, including several Grammy Awards and American Music Awards.

9 With great fame and success usually comes great wealth, and Underwood is not an exception. As a result, she has made philanthropy, or giving money to worthy causes, an important part of her life. For example, Underwood has helped her hometown community of Checotah by donating hundreds of thousands of dollars to the schools there.

10 From small town farm girl to one of the wealthiest entertainers in America, Carrie Underwood has experienced a dream come true.

**I.** Classify the following statements by writing **O** if the statement is an opinion, or **F** if the statement is a fact.

_____ Carrie Underwood's number-one hit "Inside Your Heaven" was also the best-selling single of the year.

_____ Carrie Underwood's success was largely based on the luck of winning *American Idol,* and only in small part due to her talent.

_____ Her album *Some Hearts* was the best country release of 2006.

_____ Immediately after high school, Carrie Underwood chose to attend college rather than continue pursuing a career in music.

_____ The people at Capitol Records wanted to make a record with Carrie Underwood, but circumstances changed, and the record was never made.

_____ Viewers of *American Idol*'s fourth season chose Carrie Underwood as their favorite singer.

_____ Checotah, Oklahoma, is a rural town in the eastern part of the state.

_____ In 2007, Carrie Underwood won a Grammy Award for Best New Artist.

**2.** Why does the author say that Carrie Underwood's *American Idol* win "changed her life forever"?

_____

_____

**3.** Identify three main ideas from the text. Write them on the lines below.

_____

_____

_____

_____

**4.** Choose an adjective that describes Carrie Underwood, and explain why you chose it.

_____

_____

**5.** Popular singers and other kinds of entertainers can make a tremendous amount of money. Do you think they deserve that much wealth? Why or why not?

_____

_____

# Welcome to Nashville

*What are some country music landmarks in Nashville?*

1    When Samantha Morrison's dad got a new engineering job, she and her family moved to Nashville, Tennessee. They were thrilled to arrive in their new city. The Morrisons had a week to settle into their new house and explore the town before Dad began work.

2    "There's an awful lot to see in this town," said Mr. Morrison. "What should we visit first?"

3    "If nothing else, I'd like to see the Grand Ole Opry," suggested Mrs. Morrison.

4    Samantha's brother, Alex, agreed and added, "Did you know the Grand Ole Opry started as a radio show in an office building? It became the most famous country music stage in the world, and new members of the Country Music Hall of Fame are welcomed there. Let's go on a tour!"

5    The Morrisons' visit to the Grand Ole Opry began with a short film, and then their tour guide led them backstage and through the dressing rooms. The Morrisons even visited the set of a television show filmed at the Opry. Finally, they to walked onto the Opry stage, where a six-foot circle marks the place where thousands of country music stars, including Ernest Tubb and Patsy Cline, stood to sing. Later that evening, they saw a live show.

6    "I love this place!" exclaimed Mrs. Morrison. "And they still broadcast a radio show that I can listen to!"

7    "That was amazing," said Samantha. "I can't wait until tomorrow!"

8    The next day they visited the site Samantha was most interested in seeing: the Country Music Hall of Fame. It was a huge museum, and Samantha's favorite singer had a special exhibit where some of her many gold records were displayed. Alex was fascinated by a few of the singers' cars parked inside the building. Mr. Morrison, who plays guitar, was thrilled to see the handwritten sheet music of some of the most famous songs ever written. Mrs. Morrison preferred to examine the wide range of costumes and the performers' musical instruments.

9    The next day, Alex chose to visit the Ryman Auditorium, which housed the Grand Ole Opry until 1974. The circle in the middle of the stage at the Grand Ole Opry was cut from the stage at the Ryman Auditorium. In 2010, a historic flood in Nashville damaged the Grand Ole Opry House, and the Ryman Auditorium temporarily housed the Opry once again. The tour took the Morrisons to the backstage dressing rooms and then to the Ryman Auditorium's recording studio. Alex knew visitors were allowed to record a single there if they wanted to, and he was excited to record his own personal "hit" record. Samantha followed by recording one of her own, too. The Morrisons learned about the wonderful acoustics at the Ryman Auditorium, and after attending a concert the next day, they agreed that the music played there does sound incredible. Alex declared, "That was the best concert ever!"

10    Mr. Morrison's choice is to visit RCA Studio B, a recording studio where Elvis recorded over 200 songs. Their tour guide, Mrs. Roberts, was very friendly. She let them stand on the blue "X" that marked where Elvis stood while recording his songs, and she shows them Elvis's piano as well. Mrs. Roberts told them many other interesting stories about the artists that recorded at RCA Studio B, including Charley Pride, Willie Nelson, and Dottie West.

11    After the tour, Mr. Morrison said, "That was amazing. I honestly got the feeling that the artists were still in the recording studio with us. RCA Studio B was my favorite tour in Nashville. I think we're really going to like this city!" Everyone in the family enthusiastically agreed.

**1.** Write a one-sentence summary of the text.

_____

_____

**2.** Identify two purposes the author had for writing the story.

_____

**3.** List three facts from the story.

_____

_____

_____

**4.** Choose two characters from the story, and identify what each loved seeing most.

Character: _____  Favorite thing: _____

Character: _____  Favorite thing: _____

**5.** Why were the Morrisons in Nashville? Place a checkmark on the line of the correct answer.

_____ The Morrisons took a vacation to visit the Grand Ole Opry and other sites in the city.

_____ Samantha Morrison was moving to Nashville to attend college.

_____ The family moved to Nashville because Mr. Morrison was starting a new job located there.

_____ The family was visiting Mrs. Morrison's relatives who lived in Nashville.

**6.** What is special about the circle onstage at the Grand Ole Opry?

_____

_____

**7.** Why were the Grand Ole Opry performances moved back to the Ryman Auditorium temporarily in recent years?

_____

**8.** Why do you think cultural landmarks are preserved? Are they as important as historical landmarks, such as battlefields or the birthplaces of political leaders? Explain your answer.

_____

_____

# A Perfect Storm

*What powerful forces cause a tsunami?*

1    On March 11, 2011, an earthquake occurred about 200 miles northeast of Tokyo, Japan. The earthquake registered a 9.0 magnitude on the Richter scale. This scale measures the power of earthquakes. The highest magnitude reading is 10.0. Earthquakes this powerful occur rarely, about once every 20 years. About an hour after the earthquake, waves of water from the Pacific Ocean struck Japan's coast. These 30-foot waves caused mass destruction when they crashed ashore.

2    *Tsunami* is a Japanese word. In Japanese, *tsu* means "harbor," and *nami* means "wave." But tsunamis are not isolated to Japan. About 80% of them occur within the Pacific Ocean's "Ring of Fire." Part of the Ring of Fire is an arc stretching from New Zealand to the Asian coastline. Most of the world's seismic activity occurs in this area.

3    Seismic events are shock waves that send energy through the earth. The waves result from earthquakes or explosions. In the Ring of Fire, these waves move oceanic and continental plates. When the plates break, they shift the seafloor vertically. The shift creates an energy transfer from the solid earth to the ocean waters, resulting in waves. If an earthquake occurs deep in the ocean, the tsunami's waves are often only about 1 foot high.

4    However, a tsunami changes as it nears the shoreline, where the water is shallower. The waves slow down, growing in energy and height. The *crest,* or top, of a tsunami's wave moves more rapidly than the *trough,* or bottom. This causes the seawater to rise dramatically. When the trough reaches shore, it acts like a vacuum. Coastal water recedes toward the ocean. The exposed area remaining is a critical warning sign to all that a tsunami is about to strike.

5    Following that fateful tsunami in Japan were two deadly aftershocks. These smaller earthquakes follow the *mainshock,* or what is commonly referred to as an earthquake. As a rule, the larger the earthquake, the larger the aftershocks that follow. What made the aftershocks so deadly was their location. The power of the aftershocks caused a meltdown at Fukushima Daiichi power plant.

6    Nearly 16,000 people died in the tragic aftermath of Japan's tsunami. But an even more destructive tsunami occurred on December 26, 2004, when a 9.0 earthquake occurred beneath the Indian Ocean. The rupture was more than 600 miles long. The energy released into the ocean was so great that it could have supplied power to the United States for six months. Within hours of the earthquake, a tsunami traveling at 500 miles per hour struck the coasts of 11 countries along the Indian Ocean.

7    This tsunami ranks as the fourth largest since 1900. A large tsunami had not occurred in the Indian Ocean since 1945. By the end of the day, more than 150,000 people had died or were reported missing. Thousands of miles of coastline were destroyed. Some small islands were permanently submerged. The island country of Maldives was protected by its coral reefs. Although tsunami waves washed over the entire island, the coral reefs protected it from the full force of the tsunami's effects.

8    In the aftermath of the 2004 tsunami, countries most commonly affected by tsunamis began using technology that allows them to share information about changes in air pressure and sea level. The system is so sensitive that it detects changes of about one centimeter. Seismic data is collected from monitoring stations around the world to help determine which earthquakes could cause a tsunami. Early warning may prevent tragedies such as those following the Indian Ocean and Japan tsunamis.

**I.** What is the meaning of the Japanese word *tsunami?* Place a checkmark on the line of the correct answer.

_____ wave destruction               _____ giant wave

_____ trench wave                    _____ harbor wave

**2.** What causes a tsunami? Place a checkmark on the line of the correct answer.

_____ hurricane                      _____ monsoon

_____ earthquake                     _____ typhoon

**3.** What happens along a coastline just prior to the arrival of a tsunami?

_____

**4.** What natural feature helped protect the island of Maldives when the 2004 tsunami washed over the island?

_____

**5.** What are *aftershocks*?

_____

**6.** Complete the following sentences.

The *crest* of a wave is the _____ part.

The *trough* of a wave is the _____ part.

**7.** How are nations working together to help protect each other from future tsunamis?

_____

_____

_____

**8.** The word *seismic* refers to events related to _____ .

Place a checkmark on the line of the word that best completes the above sentence.

_____ tsunamis                       _____ earthquakes

_____ wave                           _____ nuclear reactors

**9.** How could you help those who have been affected by tsunamis?

_____

_____

# A Helping Hand

*How will Jayden cope with a sudden change in his life?*

1    The soccer ball bounced loudly off Jayden's bedroom wall and ricocheted back toward his foot. As the ball reached him, he sent it flying back with a ferocious kick, and the wall shook with the impact. Jayden was furious. He wanted to send that ball smashing through the wall and into the parking lot.

2    "Jayden, cut it out!" his father yelled from down the hall. "You're going to upset the neighbors. You're mad at me, so come deal with me. Don't take it out on everyone else who lives in this building."

3    Jayden scooped up the ball as it flew back toward him, and he flopped onto his bed to stare up at the ceiling. He was so angry, he could feel tears welling up in his eyes. He knew life wasn't always fair, but sometimes it was mean.

4    Several days earlier, a major tsunami had devastated areas along the northeast coast of Japan. The powerful wave had washed ashore and traveled far inland, wiping out buildings, knocking around cars and trains, and destroying lives as it barreled along. Now, halfway around the world, the tsunami was wrecking Jayden's life as well.

5    His father, Mr. Reynolds, was a contractor, and his specialty was removing debris from demolition sites, or places where large buildings like factories had been torn down. As soon as Mr. Reynolds saw the destruction, he knew his skills could be of help to the Japanese people as they recovered from the disaster. He spent a day calling relief organizations and companies that specialized in disaster recovery. He finally located a nonprofit company that performed cleanup services after earthquakes, tornadoes, hurricanes, or, in this case, tsunamis. They told Mr. Reynolds that they could definitely use his help. He would be paid for the work, but it was a lot less than what he normally earned. In addition to the pay, the company would provide an apartment for Mr. Reynolds and his two children—meaning Jayden would live in Japan for a year.

6    As Jayden stared at his bedroom ceiling, he thought about his soccer team, his friends, his school, and everything else he would have to give up for the next year. How could his father do this to them? *Dad doesn't know anybody in Japan,* Jayden thought. *Why does he need to help them?*

7    Lying on his bed for a few minutes had helped Jayden calm down. He heaved a big sigh, sat up, and looked over to the empty suitcase on his desk, waiting there for him to start packing. Reluctantly, he opened his dresser drawer and got to work. They were leaving in the morning, and no matter how upset Jayden was, he knew he would be in the taxi headed to the airport with everyone else.

8    After he finished packing, Jayden walked down the hall to the living room, where his dad and sister were looking at images on the computer. Jayden stood behind them and looked at photographs showing piles and piles of broken material that used to be houses and other buildings. Mr. Reynolds explained that they will live a few miles from the area shown in the photos, and he would work to clean up the mess they were looking at.

9    Jayden saw that one photo showed a group of kids standing on a soggy, puddle-filled soccer field. He suddenly saw himself standing with them, and he realized how shocked and scared he would feel in the same situation. The idea that people were coming from all over the world to help fix the damage would have to make it all feel at least a little less awful. Jayden wondered if there might be something he could do to help once they got there. Maybe even playing soccer with these guys could at least take their minds off the mess for a while. By being a friend, maybe he could make life seem a little less unfair.

**I.** What details does the author include to show how angry Jayden is?

_____

_____

**2.** What does Jayden do that helps him calm down?

_____

**3.** Which of the following statements best describes the arrangement Mr. Reynolds has made with the cleanup company he will work for in Japan?

_____ Mr. Reynolds will earn a large salary and have all expenses paid while they are in Japan.

_____ Mr. Reynolds will earn a small income, and he and the family will live rent free in an apartment.

_____ Mr. Reynolds will work as a volunteer and earn no income while they are in Japan.

_____ Mr. Reynolds will pay a fee to be allowed to move to Japan and help with the clean up.

**4.** What does Mr. Reynolds' reaction to the disaster tell you about his character?

_____

_____

**5.** Compare Jayden's feelings about the move at the beginning of the story with his feelings at the end. Cite examples from the text to support your answer.

_____

_____

_____

_____

**6.** Why did Jayden's feelings change?

_____

_____

**7.** How do you react to feelings of anger? Describe any techniques you have found that help you deal with anger.

_____

# Take Cover!

*How do two brothers handle an unexpected—and dangerous—situation?*

1    Christopher grabbed the box of Wheat-Os! from the pantry, and poured himself a bowl of cereal. His older sister, Kayla, who always got home from school about half an hour earlier than he did, was already plopped down on the couch in the living room, reading a book as part of her homework. Christopher sat at the dining room table in the next room and began slurping up his afterschool snack.

2    "Dude! Could you please eat a little quieter?" Kayla called from the couch. "I can hear every bite you take!"

3    "In some cultures, it's polite to slurp," replied Christopher.

4    "Well, why don't you go enjoy your food in another culture, then?" his sister tossed back. "Preferably one far from here!"

5    Christopher kept eating—and slurping—despite his sister's comment. Their bickering back and forth was almost automatic, something they did out of habit as much as any real annoyance with each other.

6    As Christopher stared down at the milk pooled in his bowl, he saw it was trembling. At almost the same moment, he realized the entire room was vibrating. Kayla stood up suddenly and shouted, "Earthquake!"

7    The vibrations increased, and dishes began rattling loudly in the cupboards. Several books tumbled to the floor. Framed photos neatly aligned in rows around the living room walls began shifting and skewing so they hung at haphazard angles. A vase filled with fake flowers fell off its pedestal in the corner of the dining room and shattered against the ground.

8    Christopher and Kayla looked at each other and had the identical thought: *Get under the table!* Together they dove beneath the table, curled up, and covered their heads. The vibrations had continued growing, and now it felt more like giant waves rolled through the floor.

9    Christopher's eyes were tightly shut, and he prayed it would soon be over. He cracked open one eye just enough to see what his sister was doing. There was Kayla next to him, huddled in the same position. Christopher was glad to see it, because Kayla wouldn't be able to claim later on that she hadn't been scared, or say that Christopher overreacted.

10    Then, as quickly as it had begun, the shaking died away, and Christopher and Kayla slowly unfolded their bodies to sit up facing each other under the table.

11    "You all right?" Kayla asked, clearly concerned about her brother.

12    "Yeah," Christopher replied. "That was pretty scary, huh? Are you okay?"

13    Kayla nodded, and then crawled out and stood up. She felt nauseous, and her legs were unsteady; they felt like they were made of jelly. Christopher stood next to her, and they surveyed the damage around the room. In the distance, they could hear car alarms whooping and squawking, and the wailing of sirens from emergency vehicles mixed in as well. The phone rang, and they jumped, startled by the sound.

14    Christopher grabbed the receiver and pressed *Talk.* His mother was on the other end, and she let out a cry of relief to hear that her kids were not injured. Christopher described the mess the earthquake had left inside of their home, but they were both in agreement that a few damaged objects were fine compared to the kind of serious damage that could have occurred.

15    While Christopher spoke on the phone, Kayla had already started straightening the room. Christopher said goodbye to his mother, and then he retrieved a broom and dustpan from the kitchen.

16    "Man, you shoulda seen how scared you looked!" teased Christopher as he came back into the room. "What a baby!"

17    "No more a baby than you, you big baby," Kayla teased back, giving her brother a huge grin.

1. Which of the following is NOT described as an effect of the earthquake? Place a checkmark on the line of the correct answer.

   _____ windows rattling          _____ car alarms squawking

   _____ vases breaking            _____ their mother phoning

2. Why do you think Kayla feels nauseous after the earthquake?

   _____

   _____

3. The author does not state that the earthquake occurred on a school day. How do you know that it did?

   _____

   _____

   _____

4. What was the first sign that an earthquake was occurring?

   _____

5. Why does Christopher peak at his sister when they are under the table?

   _____

   _____

6. Cite evidence from the story to describe how the siblings feel about each other.

   _____

   _____

   _____

7. Write a sentence to summarize the story.

   _____

8. Why are Christopher and his mother fine with the fact that several objects broke during the earthquake?

   _____

   _____

9. Do you think hiding under the table was good decision? Why or why not?

   _____

# Designed to Last

*What does it take to help structures withstand earthquakes?*

1    Earth is made up of four layers. The top layer, or crust, contains several sheets of rocks, called *plates*. These plates are in constant, slow motion. An earthquake may occur when two of these plates suddenly slide past, move apart, or bump into each other. The seismic waves that result shake the earth, and the waves move outward, eventually shaking the ground and everything—and everyone—on it.

2    Earthquakes can cause much damage, destroying homes, bridges, and large buildings. Likewise, earthquakes can have terrible consequences for the people living in the affected area. But did you know that most injuries and deaths caused by earthquakes happen when buildings and other structures are damaged or collapse? Earth scientists and structural engineers are working hard to improve how buildings can be reinforced to survive earthquakes.

3    During ancient times, buildings were built to be incredibly stiff and strong. One example is El Castillo, a pyramid in Mexico. This pyramid was built about 1,000 years ago. It has survived numerous earthquakes. Of course, it is not possible to build structures like that nowadays. There is not enough material, and the expense would be too great. In the 1940s, scientists began to use instruments to measure how earthquakes affected structures. Over time, more and more of these instruments were installed, resulting in more accurate information.

4    In order to understand how to prevent structures from collapsing during earthquakes, scientists and engineers conduct research. As the ground beneath the structures moves, the instruments they installed gauge how effectively the structures respond. This data is used to determine how engineers can change building designs to be safer. The information is also used to improve building codes, which are rules that provide minimum standards for how to build homes, bridges, and large buildings.

5    In 1984, an earthquake in Morgan Hill, California, resulted in seismic activity that affected West Valley College, about 20 miles away. Scientists had installed instruments in the gym there. The results from the earthquake showed that the gym's roof was too flexible. If the earthquake had been any closer or any stronger, the roof might have collapsed. Afterward, the building code was revised. Large-span roofs, such as the one at West Valley College, are now built to be less flexible.

6    Engineers change how they build new structures based on building codes. But is it possible to make an existing structure safer? Engineers have also studied this problem. They realized they could retrofit, or add, features that were not considered essential when the structure was built. By retrofitting structures, engineers can help to strengthen them against the effects of earthquakes.

7    One way to retrofit is to reinforce the vulnerable joints and columns of a building or bridge. Many of the support columns in older freeway bridges in California are being reinforced with thick steel casing. This, along with cable supports between columns and roadbeds, allows freeways to survive earthquakes. A bridge's footings are also strengthened so that they are held more securely to the ground.

8    The Golden Gate Bridge in San Francisco is almost 2 miles long. The bridge spans open water. Workers have been retrofitting it since 1997 to ensure it is safer for the more than 100,000 people who use it daily. The project is currently in its third and final phase.

9    Today, instruments that measure earthquakes' effects are in bridges, dams, hospitals, and other large-scale structures. The information provided will help earth scientists and seismic engineers to design sound, safe structures in the future.

**1.** The greatest danger to human life during an earthquake is _____ .

Place a checkmark on the line of the word or phrase that best completes the sentence.

_____ seismic waves                    _____ damaged or collapsing structures

_____ damage to Earth's crust          _____ retrofitted bridges and buildings

**2.** Which of the following best describes the text's central idea? Place a checkmark on the line of the best answer.

_____ Earthquakes cause widespread damage to urban areas, where buildings and other structures are at risk of collapsing.

_____ Retrofitting older buildings increases the chance that they will remain standing and undamaged during an earthquake.

_____ Using instruments to study how buildings react to earthquakes, researchers are developing safer building methods and retrofitting older structures.

_____ Scientists are studying ancient structures that have withstood centuries of earthquakes to help them understand how to build safer modern structures.

**3.** Review the text for the meanings of the following words. Write a definition in your own words for each one.

crust: _____

building codes: _____

retrofit: _____

footings: _____

**4.** Why have some ancient structures survived numerous earthquakes? Why are buildings today not built in the same way?

_____

_____

_____

**5.** How is the text organized? Place a checkmark on the line of the best answer.

_____ time order                       _____ comparing and contrasting

_____ pros and cons                    _____ problem and solution

**6.** What natural disasters occur in your area? What kind of research do you think scientists are doing to help lessen the future impact of these events?

_____

# Wild Food

*What modern day hobby is based on a common practice in prehistoric human life?*

1    In the earliest days of human history, before the dawn of agriculture and city living, hunting and gathering were the primary means of attaining food. In fact, almost 90% of our time on Earth was spent stalking prey and wandering through the landscape to find our meals. Although farming techniques were developed about 12,000 years ago, the first humans appeared approximately 100,000 years earlier. For tens of thousands of years, our ancestors traveled the land searching for food—and nature provided plenty. Otherwise, we wouldn't be here today!

2    Foraging, or looking in nature for wild food sources, never went away completely. Nomadic tribes still exist today in a few places around the world. Nomads are people who do not settle in a permanent home. Instead, they travel throughout the year, following herds of animals or the appearance of seasonal plants in order to get food or make a living. For nomads, as well as those who live far from modern conveniences, foraging may be a necessity, but for others, foraging can be a fun hobby.

3    Edible plants grow in surprising abundance around you, even in places you might normally overlook. A weedy, abandoned lot on the next block, the woodsy area at the far end of a park, or even a backyard can each provide a variety of flavorful, nutritious foods. However, you cannot simply walk into these places, grab a handful of green, and start chomping. Modern day foragers know how risky that can be. Poisonous plants are out there, too, and sometimes it's hard to tell the difference between dangerous and delicious.

4    If you are interested in foraging, the most important rule above all others is to find an experienced adult who can guide you and make sure you are safe. They will help you identify some of the most common edible plants you will discover on an outing. These include wild onion, wild garlic, common dandelions, chickweed, red clover, brambles, stinging nettles, and the list goes on. You will also learn some other important rules that even the most experienced foragers are sure to follow.

5    First, make sure you are allowed to forage wherever it is you choose to go. Public lands, such as parks or forests, are normally fine. Sometimes there are rules you need to follow about what you can and cannot take, as well as how much you can take. If the land is privately owned, you need to get permission first to forage there; otherwise, you will be trespassing and stealing. Also, be sure to avoid places where chemicals are sprayed to kill pests or weeds.

6    Second, respect the wild places you visit. Don't leave garbage behind or damage the landscape. When you do find a patch of edible plants, be sure to take only what you need. If you gather everything, then the plant will not have a chance to grow back. It is important to the ecosystem, as well as future foragers, that you leave behind plenty of plants so they can reproduce.

7    Third, know which plants are poisonous. Although the number of plants that are poisonous enough to be fatal is small, it takes only one mistake. Many foraging field guides are available. Bringing one with you when you head into the wild can help clarify any doubts. Along with a field guide, you will want to bring a basket or other container, tools for cutting or digging, and a well stocked first aid kit.

8    Once a forager gets home with his or her bounty, it's time to prepare the meal. Again, experience makes a difference. Some wild edibles taste best raw, while others should be cooked. Cookbooks that focus on recipes for wild foods are a great place to start. Once the meal is prepared, the best part comes next: it's time to eat!

**I.** Classify the following statements as **T** if a statement is true or **F** if a statement is false.

_____ No one needs to forage for food today, but some people do it for fun anyway.

_____ For most of human history, hunting and gathering was the primary way humans got their food.

_____ Be sure to gather all of the edible plants growing in an area, because it will encourage more plants to grow back and replace the ones you took.

_____ If you decide to try foraging yourself, the most important rule is to make sure you forage on public property.

_____ Most of the plants growing in a wild environment will be highly toxic, so it is vital to have a field guide on hand.

**2.** Write a one-sentence summary for each paragraph in the text.

1. _____

2. _____

3. _____

4. _____

5. _____

6. _____

7. _____

8. _____

**3.** What evidence does the author provide to show that early humans were successful hunters and gatherers?

_____

**4.** Which statement best summarizes the author's point of view? Place a checkmark on the line of the best answer.

_____ Once humans developed agriculture, the need to hunt and gather food became obsolete.

_____ Gathering wild edible plants is a fun and rewarding hobby that also has some risks, so it is important to learn about foraging before trying it out yourself.

_____ Poisonous plants and edible plants look familiar, so it is important to purchase a field guide.

_____ Public land is usually open to foraging, but you need to be sure there are no additional rules about protected plants.

# Gathering Gifts

*How will Jackson find a gift for his mom's birthday if he's spending the day in the woods?*

1    Uncle Louis motioned with his hand, signaling for Jackson to stop. Jackson froze and looked ahead along the trail to where Uncle Louis now pointed. A large buck stood just to the left of the trail, looking backward over its shoulder to see what was coming up the path behind it. Suddenly, its antlered head swung forward, and the tan beast darted away into the thick woods.

2    "Beautiful," said Uncle Louis. They listened as the sound of the deer running through crunching leaves slowly faded away to silence. Then, Uncle Louis said, "We should take a look around the trail up there, just in case the deer was munching on something we might be able to gather."

3    They were spending Saturday morning in the woods, foraging for edible wild plants. Uncle Louis had promised Jackson that they would go foraging the next time he visited, and this weekend he was in town to be part of his sister's birthday celebration on Sunday. Uncle Louis planned to use whatever they gathered to make food for the party, and that would be his birthday gift to Jackson's mom. Jackson himself had no idea what to get his mom. As much as he was enjoying the time with his uncle, he had been distracted trying to come up with some plan for a gift.

4    As they approached the spot where the deer had stood, Uncle Louis scanned the surrounding area. Then, he stepped off the trail, headed a few feet into the woods, and stopped at a patch of plants with thin leaves and small bunches of purple flowers growing at the top. He plucked one of the leaves and stuck it into his mouth.

5    "Fireweed," he announced. "These are nice, young plants, too. This is the best time to pick them, because the leaves taste bitter when they get mature. We can eat the flowers, also. Here, try this."

6    Uncle Louis handed Jackson one of the small, purple bunches. Earlier in the morning, when Uncle Louis first started giving Jackson samples of wild plants to try, Jackson was hesitant. He would sniff the leaf, root, or flower first, and then slowly take a couple very small nibbles. But nothing so far had tasted bad or weird, and in fact, most of what he had tried tasted pretty good. So Jackson popped the flowers right into his mouth and started chewing. They had a surprisingly peppery flavor.

7    "Those will taste great mixed into a salad," said Uncle Louis. He opened the large satchel they had brought with them into the woods, and added some fireweed to the other plants that were already tucked inside: wood sorrel, dandelions, wild garlic, pennycress, and amaranth. Then, they stepped back onto the path and headed in the direction of their car.

8    As they neared the end of the trail, Uncle Louis pointed out a walnut tree. He explained that the walnuts were inside the big, green fruit-like orbs that hung from the tree and lay scattered all over the ground. He gathered a few of the green husks and told Jackson he would demonstrate later how to smash open the husk and get to the walnut inside.

9    As Uncle Louis gathered the walnut husks, Jackson spotted a large bush several yards away covered with dark, almost black berries. When he got close enough, he finally recognized something familiar to eat: blackberries! And the sight of them gave Jackson an idea.

10    "Hey, Uncle Louis, these are blackberries, right?" Jackson wanted to be sure before he ate one. As soon as his uncle confirmed the discovery, Jackson tossed one in his mouth. "Yum! It looks like Mom's getting some blackberry jam for her birthday!"

**I.** Identify the order of events by writing 1–8 on the lines.

_____ Jackson finds a blackberry bush.

_____ Jackson and Uncle Louis listen to the deer crunching through leaves.

_____ Uncle Louis explains that the green husks contain walnuts.

_____ Jackson decides to make blackberry jam for his mom's birthday.

_____ Uncle Louis finds a patch of fireweed.

_____ Uncle Louis motions for Jackson to stop.

_____ Uncle Louis sees a deer on the trail.

_____ Jackson tastes a fireweed flower.

**2.** Is this story an example of realistic fiction or fantasy? Explain your answer.

_____

_____

**3.** Do you think Uncle Louis lives near Jackson and sees him often, or does he live in another place and the two don't see each other often? How do you know?

_____

_____

_____

**4.** What is the conflict in this story? How is the conflict resolved?

_____

_____

_____

**5.** What gift will Uncle Louis give his sister for her birthday?

_____

**6.** Do you think Jackson's mom will like his gift? Why or why not?

_____

_____

**7.** Do you have a relative you like to spend time with? What do you do together?

_____

# Answer Key

**1.** Is this story fiction or nonfiction? Explain how you know.

Fiction; Kevin and the events in the story are made up by the author.

**2.** What two dishes were taught in the cooking class?

omelet        turkey Reuben

**3.** How many students were in the class altogether? Place a checkmark on the line of the correct answer.

✓ 7          _____ 11

_____ 9          _____ This information is not in the story.

**4.** Which sentence below is a direct quote by Chef Mario from story? Place a checkmark on the line of the correct answer.

✓ We'll start with a basic omelet.

_____ My omelet was fluffier because I whipped it longer with a fork.

_____ It's important to keep the coleslaw crisp and cool.

_____ Thanks for coming!

**5.** Why do you think Kevin signed up for a cooking class? Cite evidence from the story to support your answer.

Answers will vary. Possible answer: The opening sentence states that Kevin loves watching cooking shows. They probably inspired him to want to learn how to cook.

**6.** The author states that Kevin ". . . knew practice would make him better." Describe an experience of your own in which practice made you better at a particular skill.

Answers will vary.

3

**1.** Which genre of nonfiction best describes the text? Place a checkmark on the line of the correct answer.

_____ autobiography          ✓ biography

_____ historical nonfiction          _____ essay

**2.** How did the author organize the information in the text? Do you think this was a good choice? Why or why not? Answers will vary. Possible answer: The author organized the information chronologically, or in time order. This was a good choice because the text is a biography, and people live their lives in time order. It makes sense to retell the events in a person's life in time order.

**3.** Reread the focus question below the title. Write a few sentences that answer the question, based on information from the text. Answers will vary. Possible answer: Julia Child was born in America but she spent a lot of time in France and learned how to become a great French chef. Then, along with two other women, she wrote and published a book about French cooking that became a bestseller in the United States, and she hosted a cooking show called *The French Chef*.

**4.** Why did Julia Child and her co-writers have trouble publishing *Mastering the Art of French Cooking*? The book was so big, some publishers thought it was too much like an encyclopedia.

**5.** Which of the following statements is true? Place a checkmark on the line of the true statement.

_____ From the time she was young, Julia Child always dreamed of being a famous chef.

_____ Julia Child worked as a spy for the CIA during World War II.

_____ *Mastering the Art of French Cooking* was the book that inspired Julia Child to become a chef.

✓ Julia Child's first television show was called *The French Chef*.

**6.** What are you passionate about? How do you pursue your passions?

Answers will vary.

5

**1.** Identify the author's main purpose for writing the text. Place a checkmark on the line of the correct answer.

_____ entertain          _____ inform

_____ convince          ✓ explain

**2.** How does the text's organizational structure support the author's purpose? Answers will vary. Possible answer: The author's purpose is to explain the steps needed to bake bread. Organizing the steps by number helps make it clear when each step needs to be completed.

**3.** Why do you think the ingredients list is placed near the beginning of the text rather than near the end? Answers will vary. Possible answer: The ingredients are listed first so the cook can gather them and have them ready before beginning any of the steps.

**4.** Approximately how much time does the dough need to rise in total? Place a checkmark on the line of the correct answer.

_____ 3 hours          ✓ 7 hours

_____ 5 hours          _____ 10 hours

**5.** Which step occurs immediately after the third and final rising of the dough? Place a checkmark on the line of the correct answer.

_____ Shape the dough into loaves.          _____ Place the loaves into the oven.

✓ Slash the loaves diagonally.          _____ Spray the loaves with water.

**6.** Describe a time when you followed steps to complete a process. Were the steps clearly described? Was the end result a success?

Answers will vary.

7

# Answer Key

---

**Page 9**

1. Sometimes authors have more than one purpose for writing a text. Did this text have more than one purpose? Explain your answer.

   The author's purpose was to entertain and inform, because it is a fiction story, but it also contains information about severe food allergies.

2. What was Georgia allergic to? Place a checkmark on the line of the correct answer.

   _____ cranberries    ✓ peanuts

   _____ eggs    _____ milk

3. What is *anaphylaxis*? Use context clues from the text for your answer.

   Anaphylaxis is a severe allergic reaction that can cause throat swelling and difficulty breathing, as well as low blood pressure and possible loss of consciousness.

4. What is the conflict in this story? How is it resolved?

   The conflict is that the girls need to plan a menu for a hike, but two of the girls are allergic to certain foods. The conflict is resolved when Angela and Georgia explain which foods they are allergic to, and all the girls work together to prepare a menu that avoids those foods.

5. Who is Michelle? Place a checkmark on the line of the correct answer.

   _____ Georgia's best friend    ✓ scout leader

   _____ the girl who is allergic to eggs    _____ Angela's mother

6. What steps could you take to help a friend or classmate with a severe food allergy stay healthy and safe?

   Answers will vary. Possible answers might include: avoid the foods the friend is allergic to; alert the friend when the foods are in the vicinity; look up information about the allergy to learn more; share the information with the friend.

**9**

---

**Page 11**

1. Who started the Let's Move campaign? First Lady Michelle Obama

2. Which of the following is NOT one the five action steps for Let's Move? Place a checkmark on the line of the correct answer.

   _____ Drink lots of water.    _____ Try new fruits and vegetables.

   ✓ Plant a garden.    _____ Help make dinner.

3. List three ways Michelle Obama promoted the Let's Move campaign.

   1. She made TV appearances.
   2. She posted recipes online.
   3. She posted videos online.

4. Write a sentence describing the main idea of the selection.

   Answers will vary. Possible answer: Michelle Obama launched the Let's Move campaign as a way to combat childhood obesity in the United States.

5. Does the author have a positive or negative point of view about the Let's Move campaign? How do you know? Answers will vary. Possible answer: The author's point of view about Let's Move is positive. In the final paragraph, the author uses words like *helps, exciting, healthier,* and *successful* when discussing the results for children who take part in Let's Move.

6. What evidence does the author cite to support the idea that the Let's Move campaign is important?

   Answers will vary. Possible answer: The author states the statistics that one in five children is obese, and one in three is overweight.

7. Do you think the Let's Move campaign is having a positive affect on American children? Why or why not?

   Answers will vary.

**11**

---

**Page 13**

1. List the four examples of high-tech foods discussed in the text.

   3-D food printer

   edible plastic

   device that grows meat and fish

   artificial egg

2. Complete the analogy.

   *Ink tanks* are to *traditional printers* as ingredient containers are to *3-D food printers*.

3. What example does the author provide of a food technology that is common to us today, but that was once viewed as futuristic? Place a checkmark on the line of the correct answer.

   _____ eggs    _____ 3-D food printer

   ✓ frozen food    _____ bottled water

4. Write one fact presented in the text.

   Eggs help baked goods rise.

5. Write one opinion presented in the text.

   Eggless cookies or mayonnaise tastes no different than ones made with chicken eggs.

6. Does the author provide a balanced and unbiased point of view about the future foods covered in the text? Explain your answer.

   Answers will vary. Possible answer: The author does not present a completely unbiased point of view. All of the examples are described in a positive way, and no cons are provided about any of them. For example, plastic packaging often protects food from germs, so what protects the edible plastic packaging from getting dirty?

7. Imagine a future food technology that has not been developed. Write a few sentences describing what you imagine. How does this technology benefit people?

   Answers will vary

**13**

---

# Answer Key

---

**1.** Which of the following is NOT included in the story as something Madison and her family saw at the Renaissance Fair?

✓ a group of medieval singers      _____ a tightrope walker

_____ a fire eater      _____ fake weapons

**2.** Besides cash registers and credit card machines, list three other kinds of modern equipment that would most likely be part of a Renaissance Fair.

Answers will vary. Possible answers: port-a-potties refrigerators for drinks or food electricity

**3.** Explain what *jousting* is.

Men riding horses and carrying lances try to knock each other off their horses.

**4.** Why does Madison choose not to ride on the merry-go-round?

She felt dizzy after riding the merry-go-round the year before.

**5.** In your own words, describe the meaning of *manual* based on how the word is used to describe the merry-go-round.

Answers may vary. Possible answer: The merry-go-round is not powered by a machine, it is powered by people pushing it around, so *manual* means powered by hand, not by machine.

**6.** Why do you think the King and Queen are often a couple who have been part of the fair for many years? Explain your answer.

Answers will vary. Possible answer: It would be a big honor to be the King and Queen of the fair, so voters want to pick a couple of people who deserve the honor. A couple who have been part of the fair for many years would make a good choice.

**7.** The people at a Renaissance Fair dress up and reenact what life might have been like in medieval times. If you could choose a different time period to have people reenact, what would it be? Describe details of what would be included in the reenactment, including what people might wear or do.

Answers will vary.

**15**

---

**1.** Classify the following statements by writing **O** if the statement is an opinion, or **F** if the statement is a fact.

O   Merian's stepfather created beautiful still lives.

O   Amsterdam, Netherlands, was the best city Merian could have chosen to move to.

F   The hot and humid jungles of Suriname provided many different kinds of insects for Merian to observe.

O   The most important event in Merian's life was traveling to Suriname.

F   The main focus of much of Merian's work was studying the process of metamorphosis.

F   After being somewhat forgotten for many centuries, the work of Maria Merian was rediscovered during the 20th century.

**2.** What is *metamorphosis*? A process of transformation, such as when a caterpillar changes into a moth or butterfly.

**3.** What made Amsterdam a good place for Merian to move to?

Merian was a single woman, and since Amsterdam was a city where women could own their own property and businesses, she would be able to make a living there.

**4.** Identify the sentence in the first paragraph that presents the main idea of the text. Write the sentence below. Centuries ago, at a time when most women had little independence or power over their lives, Maria Merian used her artistic skills and knowledge of the natural world to achieve great success.

**5.** Does the author present sufficient evidence and details in the text to support the main idea? Explain your answer. The author mostly supports the main idea. The author shows that Merian was a skilled artist and naturalist, and she had great business success with her gallery. However, she does have "great success" with her Suriname book, because other scientists criticized it.

**6.** Do you think Merian's gender played a role in the scientists' criticisms of her work? Why or why not? Answers will vary. Possible answer: Her gender probably played some role, because nearly all of the scientists then were men. They may have thought she couldn't be a good scientist because she was a woman, and so they were less likely to trust what she had painted.

**17**

---

**1.** What was the most common food in Medieval Europe? Place a checkmark on the line of the correct answer.

_____ beef      ✓ bread

_____ chicken      _____ broth

**2.** Why were spices a luxury? Transportation of goods was slow and expensive, and spices came from far away, so spices were expensive.

**3.** Why were towels provided during medieval feasts?

People ate mostly with their hands, so towels were used to keep their hands clean.

**4.** Complete the following statement.

Noblewomen often ate separately from men because Eating was messy and noblewomen weren't supposed to be seen getting messy.

**5.** Why did nobility avoid eating breakfast?

Breakfast was seen as unnecessary and indulgent for people who did not do physical labor.

**6.** Which of the following was NOT a detail described in the text? Place a checkmark on the line of the correct answer.

_____ A middle class emerged during the Middle Ages.

_____ What people ate was largely determined by their economic level in society.

✓ For the most part, clergy and nobility were allowed to eat the same types of foods.

_____ Different kinds of foods were eaten in specific order to help with digestion.

**7.** Think about the last meal you ate, including the food, the setting, and the etiquette. How was it similar to and different from a meal during the Middle Ages?

Answers will vary.

**19**

---

# Answer Key

---

**Page 21**

1. Which point of view is used in telling this story: first-person, second-person, or third-person? Explain how you know.

   The story is told in first-person point of view. The narrator uses the pronouns I, my, and we, which indicates that the story is told from the narrator's point of view.

2. Identify the order of events in the story by writing 1–8 on the lines.

   3 Dan and Brandon get a drink of water.

   8 Megan gives Dan and Brandon a pamphlet about archery lessons.

   7 Dan misses the target.

   4 Megan shares a little bit about the history of archery.

   6 Brandon hits the edge of the target with his arrow.

   2 Dan and Brandon see men and women shooting arrows.

   5 Brandon drops his arrow.

   1 Dan and Brandon attend a Medieval Festival.

3. What is the story's setting?

   place: a Medieval Festival    time: now

4. Although Dan misses the target when he tried to shoot an arrow, he decides to take archery classes with Brandon. What does this tell you about Dan?

   Answers will vary. Possible answer: Dan is not a quitter, and he knows he needs to practice if he wants to learn a new skill.

5. Describe a time when you failed at a new skill. How did you feel? Did you try to get better?

   Answers will vary.

**21**

---

**Page 23**

1. Who is the main character of this story? Place a checkmark on the line of the correct answer.

   _____ Berylbridge Castle    ✓ Brandon Mackey

   _____ Mr. Mackey    _____ the tour guide

2. Explain the purpose of a drawbridge.

   A drawbridge helps people get across the moat to enter the castle. It can also be raised to close the entrance to the castle and eliminate a way to easily cross the moat.

3. According to the text, how does a moat help protect a castle?

   A moat makes it difficult to get near the castle's walls. If it has water, an attacker would need to swim across the moat. If it has no water, the attacker still needs to climb down into the ditch and back up the other side. Either way, the attacker is vulnerable to the archers positioned on the walls and towers of the castle.

4. What is this text mostly about?

   _____ Brandon's feelings about the car ride    ✓ the purpose and structure of castles

   _____ Brandon's enjoyment of the tour    _____ the purpose of the keep

5. How would this text have been different if it were nonfiction explanatory text?

   Answers will vary. Possible answer: The text would not have a fictional family, and it would not include elements such as the description of a car ride to the castle or a tour guide explaining about the castle. The text would probably also have no quotation marks.

6. Have you taken a tour of a historical site or other kind of place? Write a short paragraph comparing the tour you took with the tour Brandon takes in the story.

   Answers will vary.

**23**

---

**Page 25**

1. Why might some people find it surprising that Jim Abbott was a successful professional baseball player?

   He had only one fully functioning hand.

2. Why did Jim Abbott choose not to use a prosthetic hand?

   When he was young, he found it too uncomfortable and decided it was more trouble than it was worth.

3. Which of the following is NOT a team Jim Abbott played with? Place a checkmark on the line of the correct answer.

   _____ Michigan Wolverines    ✓ Cleveland Indians

   _____ California Angels    _____ New York Yankees

4. In your own words, explain how Jim Abbott was able to pitch, catch, and throw using only one hand.

   When he pitched, he balanced the glove on his right arm. As soon as he threw the ball, he grabbed the glove and put it on so he would be ready to catch the ball. As soon as he caught the ball, he removed the glove and tucked it along with the ball under his arm, grabbed the ball out with his good hand, and threw it.

5. The author believes that Jim Abbott was a successful baseball player. What evidence does the author cite to support this idea? Do you agree with the author? Why or why not?

   Answers will vary. Possible answer: The author lists Jim Abbott's accomplishments in baseball, which include playing in the college World Series, playing for the U.S. Olympic team, and pitching a no-hitter. I agree with the author that Jim Abbott was successful, because these accomplishments are greater than what many professional baseball players achieve.

6. Despite physical challenges that could be frustrating at times, Jim Abbott refused to feel sorry for himself and never quit trying his best to succeed. Write a description of someone you know who shares one or both of these attributes.

   Answers will vary.

**25**

---

# Answer Key

---

**1.** Which two teams played in the 1919 World Series?

_Chicago White Sox_ against _Cincinnati Reds_

**2.** Why were the players unhappy?

The were underpaid for their skills, and teammates were not equally paid.

**3.** Complete the following sentence.

If a player wanted to quit one team to go play for another team, first he had to

ask permission from the owner to get out of the contract.

**4.** What type of writing was this text? Place a checkmark on the line of the best answer.

_____ biography          ✓ historical nonfiction

_____ historical fiction          _____ persuasive essay

**5.** The author describes three main elements that led to the Black Sox Scandal. What are they?

The players were underpaid. The owner of the White Sox was too greedy to pay them fairly. Gamblers tempted them with money.

**6.** Do you think it was fair that the players involved in the scandal were banned from baseball for life? Why or why not?

Answers will vary.

**7.** Fables are fictional stories that often teach a lesson. They usually end with a moral, or a short statement that summarizes the lesson. What lesson do you think could be taught with this story? Write a moral to the story of the Black Sox Scandal.

Answers will vary.

27

---

**1.** In your own words, describe the meaning of each word, based on how it is used in the story. Answers will vary. Possible answers shown.

skepticism: The word is used to describe Matt and Zachary as they wonder about whether Victor can play or not, so the word means "doubtful," wondering, or questioning.

particularly: The word is used when Victor is talking about what he loves about baseball, and it describes what he specifically loves most, so it means in a specific way.

product: A product is something you produce, or make, but the author uses the word to describe what is made when you multiply two things together, like the answer to a multiplication problem.

**2.** What sentence best describes the theme of this story? Place a checkmark next to the best answer.

_____ Wheelchair baseball is no different than traditional baseball.

✓ A person in a wheelchair can be a great athlete.

_____ Batting is the best part of playing baseball.

_____ Baseball combines mathematics and physics for fun.

**3.** Why were Matt and Zachary impressed?

They weren't sure whether someone in a wheelchair could play baseball, but Victor turned out to be a great hitter.

**4.** Why did Victor play catcher instead of heading to the outfield?

Since Victor is in a wheelchair, he would have trouble being mobile through the grass or rough ground of the outfield.

**5.** Why do batters in wheelchair baseball sometimes attach their wheelchairs to a metal frame?

When a batter swings hard, the force of the swing might move or even knock over the wheelchair.

**6.** In addition to what is explained in the story, describe two other ways that you think a wheelchair baseball game would differ from a traditional baseball game.

Answers will vary. Possible answer: All the players would be wheeling instead of running. There would be no grass.

29

---

**1.** What is a *conservationist*? Use the text to help you write a definition.

A person who works to protect the natural environment.

**2.** Classify the following statements from the text by writing **O** if the statement is an opinion, or **F** if the statement is a fact.

_F_ It is estimated that within 50 years, 30% of all land, marine, and fresh-water animals will be extinct.

_O_ An interesting fact about DNA is that it is capable of making copies of itself.

_F_ Knowing about an animal's DNA gives clues to its ecological needs.

_F_ The frozen cells can be stored safely for up to 100 years.

_O_ The professionals involved in the project are very qualified.

_F_ Climate change, illegal trade, and over-fishing are other causes that can lead to a species' extinction.

**3.** What is the author's purpose for writing this text? Place a checkmark on the line of the best answer.

_____ to entertain          _____ to persuade

✓ to inform          _____ to explain

**4.** Is it harmful to the animals to collect DNA samples from them? Explain your answer.

It is not harmful, because the samples can be taken from hair, feathers, or feces that are not even attached to the animal.

**5.** Where does the Frozen Ark Project get its name? Place a checkmark on the line of the correct answer.

_____ The DNA samples are stored at a research facility located in Antarctica.

_____ The project is sponsored by Frozen Ark Foods, Inc.

✓ The project freezes animal cells to preserve their DNA.

_____ Scientists are concerned about mass extinctions that could result from a new ice age.

**6.** List three of the benefits provided by the Frozen Ark Projects.

It can help preserve animals that end up becoming extinct. It can help scientists study toxins in the animals' environments. It can help scientists monitor the genetics in a population of animals to be sure they are healthy.

Spectrum Reading Grade 7

31

---

# Answer Key

---

**1.** How does Kayla learn about the threat to the manatees' habitat? She read about the housing development in a newspaper article.

**2.** What are the two parts of Kayla's plan?
First, Kayla and her classmates will hold a fundraiser for a local wildlife group. Second, Kayla will meet with the developer and encourage him or her to institute a boat speed limit in the river.

**3.** List three characteristics of manatees described in the story.
Answers will vary. Possible answers: Manatees like warm water. Manatees like to eat sea grass. Manatees have flippers.

**4.** Why is the setting important in this story?
Manatees don't live everywhere, so the story has to be set in a place where manatees live. If the story were set in Alaska, it would not make sense.

**5.** What does Kayla mean by the statement, *I guess human activities aren't always bad for the manatees?* Answers will vary.
Possible answer: The activity of the students will be to hold a fundraiser to help save the manatees' habitat, so it will benefit the manatees and not harm them.

**6.** Do you think Kayla's plan will work? Why or why not?
Answers will vary.

**7.** What animals are common where you live? Describe how human activities might affect the habitats of these animals.
Answers will vary.

**33**

---

**1.** Which point of view is used in telling this story: first-person, second-person, or third-person? Explain how you know. The story is told in third-person. The author uses pronouns such as *he*, *they*, and *their* and the narrator is not any of the characters in the story.

**2.** Identify the order of events in the story by writing 1–8 on the lines.

7 The rescuers wrapped the injured manatee in a net.

5 Mr. Jones radioed the Wildlife Rescue Patrol.

1 Mr. Jones caught a kingfish.

4 Tyler and Mr. Jones saw the injured manatee.

8 The rescuers dragged the manatee onto the boat.

6 Mr. Jones radioed his wife to say he and Tyler would be late.

3 Tyler saw blood in the water.

2 The speedboat raced past Tyler and Mr. Jones.

**3.** The author wrote "the speedboat came flying up the river . . . " Explain why this is an example of figurative language, rather than a literal, or actual, description of what happened. Answers will vary. Possible answer: The boat was not literally flying; the author used the word *flying* to emphasize how fast the boat was travelling.

**4.** As Mr. Jones approaches the mouth of the Longtooth River, he slows down. Why do you think he does this?
Mr. Jones knows there are manatees swimming in the water along the coast and in the river, so he goes slowly to be sure he doesn't injure any of them.

**5.** The author never explicitly states what time of day the story takes place, so how do you know? Cite evidence from the text to support your answer.
The author describes the sun blazing high in the sky, and Tyler and his father are on their way home after fishing all morning, so the story takes place in the afternoon.

**6.** What do Mr. Jones's and Tyler's actions tell you about them? Cite evidence from the text to support your answer. Answers will vary. Possible answer: Mr. Jones slows down the boat to avoid harming manatees; Tyler loves looking for manatees; Mr. Jones calls the rescuers to come help an injured manatee; so Mr. Jones and Tyler care about manatees and protecting them.

**35**

---

**1.** In your own words, explain why Diwali is called "The Festival of Lights."
Diwali is called "The Festival of Lights" because Hindis traditionally light lamps or other lights for holiday to attract the goddess Lakshmi so she will bring them good luck for the coming year.

**2.** Who is Lakshmi? Place a checkmark on the line of the best answer.

✓ the goddess of wealth      _____ the goddess of light

_____ the goddess of the new year      _____ the goddess of positivity

**3.** Use context clues to define each of the following terms from the text:
sari: a long, colorful fabric that women wear wrapped around their bodies like a dress

sag paneer: a spinach and cheese dish

mithai: sweet and savory snacks

rangoli: a design made from colored powders

kurta: a long, collarless shirt

**4.** What nation did Dev's ancestors most likely come from? Place a checkmark on the line of the best answer.

_____ Egypt      _____ England

✓ India      _____ Japan

**5.** Choose an adjective that you think describes Dev. Support your choice with evidence from the story.
Answers will vary. Possible answer: Dev is generous, because he is hurrying home at the beginning of the story so he can help get ready for the party, and because he brings snacks upstairs to his dog at the end.

**6.** What cultural holiday or tradition is most important to you? Describe what it is and why it is important to you.
Answers will vary.

**37**

---

# Answer Key

---

**1.** Which of the genres listed below best describes the text? Place a checkmark on the line of the best choice.

✓ biography          _____ historical nonfiction

_____ autobiography        _____ historical fiction

**2.** Classify the following statements as **T** if a statement is true or **F** if a statement is false.

F "Mahatma" is an honorable title meaning *truth force*.

T Gandhi was born in India, attended college in England, and lived much of his life in South Africa.

F Gandhi wore simple clothes because he was born into a lower caste.

F The powerful salt march protest marked the end of British rule in India.

**3.** The author describes Gandhi as one of the 20th century's most important leaders. What evidence does the author cite to support this idea?

Answers will vary. Possible answer: The author describes the protests Gandhi led in South Africa that resulted in major changes in the laws there. The author tells how Gandhi's actions in India led to the end of British rule there.

**4.** Why did Gandhi dislike the title "Mahatma"?

Being called "Mahatma" was an important honor, but Gandhi preferred to be seen as a regular, simple person.

**5.** Based on what you've read about Gandhi, choose three words to describe him. Explain why you chose each word.     Answers will vary. Possible answers shown.

1. determined. Even though he was jailed many times and faced great odds, he never gave up.

2. generous. He could have chosen to do other things with his life, but he chose to dedicate it to helping others.

3. brave. He stood up to powerful people and never backed down.

**39**

---

**1.** What is the main idea of the passage? Place a checkmark next to the sentence that most closely describes them main idea of the passage.

_____ Humans illegally hunt, farm, and collect timber from the Sundarbans.

_____ The Sundarban Reserve Forest is the largest mangrove forest on Earth.

✓ The Sundarban Reserve Forest is a unique and important environmental site that needs to be protected.

_____ Mangrove forests support an amazingly diverse number of plants and animals, and they help reduce erosion of the coastline.

**2.** On the lines below, write three facts about mangrove forests.

1. Mangrove forests grow in slow-moving waters.

2. The dense root structure of a mangrove forest helps prevent erosion.

3. The dense roots also provide protection for many animals.

**3.** What does UNESCO stand for? United Nations Educational, Scientific, and Cultural Organization

**4.** Describe the author's viewpoint about mangrove forests. Use evidence from the text to support your answer. Answers will vary. Possible answer: The author believes mangrove forests are important places that deserve to be protected. The author makes this clear by describing all the good things mangrove forests do for animals and the land, including listing how many different kinds of animals rely on the forests.

**5.** Write three sentences summarizing the second paragraph.

1. Mangrove forests are found mostly near the equator.

2. The dense roots help protect the coastline from erosion.

3. Mangrove forests are homes to a wide variety of animals.

**6.** Describe a natural environment that is important or special to you, such as a park, nature preserve, or other outdoor place. What makes it a special place?

Answers will vary.

**7.** If you learned that this special place was threatened by development, what do you think you could to help protect it?

Answers will vary.

**41**

---

**1.** The Taj Mahal is a real place, and Shah Jahan and Mumtaz Mahal were real people. Which of the following genres of writing best describes the text? Place a checkmark on the line of the best answer.

_____ fable          ✓ historical nonfiction

_____ folk tale       _____ biography

As indicated, provide either a cause or an effect to complete each cause-and-effect relationship below. There may be more than one possible answer, but the cause or effect you provide must make sense according to events in story.

**2. cause:** Prince Khurran sees Arjumand Banu Begum at the market.

**effect:** The prince sends a guard over to profess his love and learn her name.

**3. cause:** Prince Khurran becomes the emperor, so Arjumand Banu Begum is the empress.

**effect:** Arjumand Banu Begum is renamed Mumtaz Mahal.

**4. cause:** Mumtaz Mahal dies during childbirth.

**effect:** Shah Jahan orders the construction of the Taj Mahal.

**5.** Provide your own example of a c.. Answers will vary. Possible answer:

**cause:** Prince Khurran visits Arjumand's father to ask his permission to marry her.

**effect:** Arjumand's father says he must wait for a while before they can marry.

**6.** Reread the story. the author, and w.. Answers will vary. Possible answers shown.

Fact: Prince Khurran was the grandson of Akbar the Great.

Fact: Prince Khurran became the Mughal Emperor Shah Jahan

Fact: The Taj Mahal was built as a monument to Mumtaz Mahal.

Fiction: Prince Khurran walking through the market.

Fiction: Prince Khurran sent a guard over to profess his love.

Fiction: The guards were worried about Prince Khurran's reaction when he sees Arjumand.

**7.** Explain how you determined which parts were fact and which were fiction.

Answers will vary. Possible answer: The beginning of the story includes a lot of details about Prince Khurran and how he met Arjumand. These are most likely made up. The facts about who built the Taj Mahal and why it was built are mostly likely true.

**43**

---

# Answer Key

---

**1.** What does *HSAM* stand for? Place a checkmark on the line of the correct answer.

_____ highly selective automatic memory

__✓__ highly superior autobiographical memory

_____ highly specialized aptitude for memorization

_____ highly selective analysis of memorization

**2.** Based on information in the text, which of the following conclusions could you draw? Place a checkmark on the line of the best answer.

_____ People with HSAM often work in fields such as astrophysics, neuroscience, or theoretical mathematics.

__✓__ People with HSAM have an unusual ability to remember events and experiences from their lives, but they are not necessarily more intelligent than all other people.

_____ People with HSAM have an unusual ability to remember events and experiences from their lives, but they have difficulty remembering facts that are unrelated to their personal experiences.

_____ People with HSAM have more negative experiences in their lives, often due to their unique ability to remember so much.

**3.** Why does the author write, *Sometimes forgetting isn't such a bad thing?*

Answers will vary. Possible answer: All of us have bad experiences in our lives. If we can forget about them, we can move on and they won't have any affect on the present.

**4.** In your own words, explain the difference between white matter and gray matter in the brain.

Answers will vary. Possible answer: White matter is the part of the brain where learning takes place. Gray matter is the part of the brain where thinking happens.

**5.** The author states that some researchers wonder if HSAM is the result of physical changes in the brain that occur in childhood. What evidence is provided to show that this idea is a possibility?

The author describes how researchers have shown that the brains of children who take music lessons change physically.

**6.** Imagine you have HSAM. Describe one positive result of having HSAM. Then, describe one negative result.

Answers will vary.

**45**

---

**1.** Is this story fiction or nonfiction? How do you know? Fiction. Even though the story contains real information about Alzheimer's disease, the characters and the events are made up by the author.

**2.** What is the author's main purpose? Support your answer with evidence from the text.

Answers may vary. Possible answer: Even though this is a fiction story, the author included a lot of details about the symptoms of Alzheimer's disease, so the author's main purpose is to share information about Alzheimer's disease.

**3.** What details does the author include to show that Mrs. Pellegrino has Alzheimer's disease?

The author shows Mrs. Pellegrino lost and confused a block away from her home. She does not remember how to get back home, even though it is so close.

**4.** Which of the following is NOT included in the text as a symptom of Alzheimer's disease? Place a checkmark on the line of the correct answer.

_____ memory loss      __✓__ more likely to be injured

_____ changes in personality      _____ withdrawal from social activities

**5.** Who is Charlotte? Place a checkmark on the line of the correct answer.

_____ Esperanza's mom      _____ Mrs. Pellegrino's daughter

__✓__ Mrs. Pellegrino's cat      _____ Mrs. Pellegrino's first name

**6.** How will Esperanza help Mrs. Pellegrino? She will visit after school sometimes to help run errands and do chores.

**7.** What does the story tell you about Esperanza?

Answers will vary. Possible answer: Esperanza is a generous and kind person who takes time to help her neighbor.

**8.** Why is it important to help our neighbors? Describe something you have done or plan to do to help one of your neighbors.

Answers will vary.

**47**

---

**1.** Which of the following is NOT a suggestion from the text for improving your memory?

_____ Eat the right foods.      __✓__ Take memory enhancing pills.

_____ Get enough sleep.      _____ Use memory tools.

**2.** Write a sentence summarizing the main idea of the text.

Answers will vary. Possible answer: Having a good memory is helpful in all aspects of life, and there are several ways to help improve your memory.

**3.** Why does the author say relaxing can help improve your memory?

Stress has a negative effect on your ability to remember things, so learning to relax can help.

**4.** The paragraphs in the text are organized as a bulleted list. Why do you think the author chose to organize the text this way? Do you think this was or was not a good way to organize the information? Explain your answer.

Answers will vary. Possible answer: The author organized the suggestions as a bulleted list because the order was not important. Each tip can be read by itself, so there was no need to organize the information in paragraphs that flow together. I think this was a good way to organize the information, because I was able to the read the tips that looked most interesting first.

**5.** Create a sentence to use as a mnemonic device for remembering the names of the original Thirteen Colonies: Delaware, Pennsylvania, New Jersey, Georgia, Connecticut, Massachusetts, Maryland, South Carolina, North Carolina, New Hampshire, Virginia, New York, Rhode Island.

Answers will vary. Possible answer shown.
Drive Past New Jersey to Go Crazy Making Money in the Carolinas, but Never Visit New York Island.

**6.** Which two suggestions from the text would be easiest for you to put into practice first? Explain why.

Answers will vary.

**49**

---

# Answer Key

---

**1.** Why does the author set the characters' names in boldface?
When a name is set in boldface, it indicates which character is speaking the words that follow.

**2.** What is the purpose of having some words set in regular font and some words set in italics? The words in regular font are the words being spoken by the characters. The words in italics are descriptions of what the characters are doing.

**3.** Why do you think the author chose to present the text in this form, rather than using paragraphs and quotation marks? Since the text describes an interview between Frederick and his grandfather, the most important part of the story is the dialogue, so it makes sense to present the story as a play.

**4.** Why is Frederick interviewing Grandpa Davison?
The interview is a school assignment.

**5.** Complete the sentence below.
Grandpa Davidson's family moved from the city to the country because  Doctors said it would be good for his brother's asthma.

**6.** Write a short paragraph summarizing Grandpa Davidson's description of his youth.
Answers will vary. Possible answer shown: Grandpa Davidson lived on a farm with his family, and everyone in the family pitched in to help run it. The work was hard, but they also had fun. Grandpa Davidson loved sledding in the winter. He also like bringing their animals to the state fair each year. Their animals won many blue ribbons at the fair.

**7.** What relative would you most like to interview? Why?
Answers will vary.

**8.** Write three questions that you would ask your relative in an interview.
1. Answers will vary.
2. _____
3. _____

**51**

---

**1.** Complete the timeline below by including a description of an event from Norman Rockwell's life that corresponds to each date. Refer to the text as needed.

1894: Norman Rockwell is born.
1908: Rockwell starts art school.
1915: Rockwell and his family move to New Rochelle.
1916: Rockwell illustrates his first *Saturday Evening Post* cover.
1920: Rockwell illustrates his first calendar for the Boy Scouts.
1939: Rockwell is awarded the Silver Beaver medal by the Boy Scouts.
1943: Rockwell paints his *Four Freedoms* series.
1964: Rockwell paints *The Problem We All Live With*.
1977: Rockwell dies.

**2.** Why did readers look forward to Rockwell's illustration for the first *Saturday Evening Post* of April each year? The cover had hidden "April Fool's" details that were fun to search for.

**3.** What influence did Norman Rockwell have on America during World War II? Cite evidence from the text in your answer. Answers may vary. Possible answer: By creating and displaying the *Four Freedoms* paintings, Rockwell was able to help the nation raise $130 million to put toward the effort of fighting World War II.

**4.** Explain why someone might look at a photograph of a Thanksgiving gathering and compare it to a Norman Rockwell painting. Answers may vary. Possible answer: Rockwell's *Freedom from Want* painting is one of the most famous images of Thanksgiving, so when people see a picture of their own families gathered for Thanksgiving, it reminds them of Rockwell's painting.

**5.** What is *The Problem We All Live With* that Rockwell refers to in the title of his painting?
racism

**6.** Why was Rockwell awarded the Silver Beaver by the Boy Scouts?
to honor his many years as an illustrator for both *Boys' Life* and the Boy Scout calendars

**53**

---

As indicated, provide either a cause or an effect to complete each cause-and-effect relationship below. There may be more than one possible answer, but the cause or effect you provide must make sense according to events in the story.

**1. cause:** Abigail is asked to clean out her grandmother's garage.
**effect:** She finds what she thinks is a Norman Rockwell painting.

**2. cause:** Abigail pulls a large box of sports equipment away from the wall.
**effect:** She sees the painting leaning against the wall.

**3. cause:** Abigail thinks she found a Norman Rockwell painting.
**effect:** Abigail calls Grandma Louise.

**4. cause:** Abigail sees that the painting is signed *Norman Rockwell.*
**effect:** Abigail shouts, "Norman Rockwell!"

**5.** Provide your own example of a cause-and-effect relationship from the story.
**cause:** Answers will vary.
**effect:**

**6.** Does this story take place in the past, present, or future? Explain your answer.
The story does not take place in the past, because Amy uses a computer to search the Internet. The author does not include anything futuristic either, so the story most likely takes place in the present.

**7.** Why does Abigail decide the painting is still a "treasure," even though it is not a real Norman Rockwell painting?
Her grandfather painted the picture, so it has sentimental value to her, even if it is not valuable in terms of money.

**8.** What object is important and valuable to you, even though it may not have monetary value? What makes it valuable?
Answers will vary.

**55**

---

Spectrum Reading Grade 7

**139**

# Answer Key

**1.** Identify the sentence in the second paragraph that summarizes the main idea of text. Write it on the line below. Scientists take several factors into consideration as they plan meals for space.

**2.** What evidence does the author provide to support the main idea? Cite specific examples from the text in your answer. The author specifies the considerations for space food. The author describes how nutrition and taste determine which kinds of foods will be prepared. The author then explains that how the food is packaged is also important, because the packaging needs to be light, and it needs to be secure.

**3.** Which of the following is least likely to be supplied as a food choice for astronauts on a spacecraft? Place a checkmark on the line of the best answer.

_____ banana      ✓ canned soup

_____ pita chips      _____ burrito

**4.** Which of the following is NOT described in the text as a consideration when determining which foods to bring on a space mission? Place a checkmark on the line of the correct answer.

_____ nutrition      _____ weight

✓ cost      _____ taste

**5.** Why are most of the meals sent into space first dehydrated and then vacuum-sealed in plastic packaging? Dehydrated and tightly-sealed foods will last a long time without spoiling.

**6.** How does the lack of gravity in the spacecraft affect how foods are served? Foods must be served in containers that keep them from floating around in the cabin, and the containers must be attached to trays.

**7.** What is your favorite meal? Would it be available during spaceflight? Explain why or why not. Answers will vary.

---

**1.** Which of the following statements best summarizes the author's point of view? Place a checkmark on the line of the best answer.

_____ Because of radiation and other dangers, studying twins in space is a risky endeavor.

✓ Studying twins in space will result in research that benefits future astronauts as well as people on Earth.

_____ Mark and Scott Kelly are brave astronauts willing to put their lives in danger to benefit humankind.

_____ Mark will participate as an observational subject, but without a control subject, the results of the twin mission will not be very helpful.

**2.** Why are twins good candidates for a study on the effects of space travel? Answers may vary. Possible answer: Because twins are so much alike physically, one of them is like the control in an experiment, while the other is the experiment.

**3.** Which of the following is NOT described in the text as a focus of the study? Place a checkmark on the line of the correct answer.

_____ the effects of space travel on DNA

✓ the maximum amount of time a human can survive in space

_____ the way bacteria in the body are affected by space travel

_____ psychological affects of living in space

**4.** Which of the following statements is true? Write T on the line of the true statement.

_____ Neither Mark nor Scott Kelly has traveled to space before.

_____ Mark has traveled to space in the past, but Scott has not.

_____ Scott has traveled to space in the past, but Mark has not.

T Both Scott and Mark Kelly have traveled to space before.

**5.** Why do you think NASA asks for a large number of proposals for studies, but then chooses only a small number of them to actually fund and complete? Answers may vary. Possible answer: By asking for a lot of proposals, NASA has the chance to see a lot of ideas and make sure they are focusing on the best type of research.

**6.** Do you think a manned mission to Mars will occur in your lifetime? Why or why not? Answers will vary.

---

**1.** Is this story an example of realistic fiction? Why or why not? Yes, this story is realistic fiction because it describes characters and events that could happen in real life, including Space Camp, which is a real place.

**2.** Which of the following is NOT an activity Jessica did at space camp? Place a checkmark on the line of the correct answer.

_____ watch a 3-D movie about the space program

_____ design, build, and launch a rocket

✓ ride in a machine that simulates what it feels like to be launched into space

_____ design a biology experiment that might be conducted on the ISS

**3.** Classify the following statements as **T** if a statement is true or **F** if a statement is false.

F Jessica loves experiencing what it feels like to be on the moon.

T Jessica's partner for the week is her dorm roommate, Jan.

T Neither Jessica nor Jan plan to visit Mars if the chance ever comes.

F Jan's rocket comes in first place at the launch competition, and Jessica feels disappointed that her rocket didn't win.

T Jessica would like to be an astronaut someday.

**4.** Why is Friday described as "the big day"? Friday is the day of the rocket launch competition.

**5.** Why are Jan and Jessica glad they worked hard in math class? Designing and building the rocket requires a lot of precise math, so they are both glad they understand math.

**6.** Would you like to attend space camp? Why or why not? Answers will vary.

**7.** Would you be willing to take part in a manned mission to Mars? Why or why not? Answers will vary.

# Answer Key

**1.** Classify each of the following statements by writing **O** if the statement is an opinion or **F** if the statement is a fact.

  O  The Tunguska Event was the most important scientific event in Russia during the 20th century.

  F  Most of the Chelyabinsk asteroid was destroyed when it exploded.

  F  Our solar system contains millions of asteroids that vary greatly in size.

  O  Meteor showers provide dazzlingly beautiful streaks of light across the night sky.

  O  Most likely, scientists will be unable to identify the next asteroid heading toward Earth.

  F  The Chelyabinsk asteroid was estimated to be about 65 feet in diameter.

**2.** What can you infer about the scientists who found the one-ton piece of meteorite or the work they did to retrieve it from the bottom of a frozen lake? Write your inference below.
Answers will vary. Possible answer: The scientists had some way of knowing where to look for the meteorite, either because someone saw where it landed or they searched the most likely area where meteorites would have landed and saw a big hole in the frozen lake's surface.

**3.** Write a short paragraph comparing and contrasting asteroids, meteoroids, meteors, and meteorites.
Answer may vary. Possible answer: Meteoroids and asteroids are both objects orbiting through our solar system, but meteoroids are much smaller than asteroids. A meteor is not a physical object at all; it is the light given off when an object burns up in the atmosphere. A meteorite is rock or metal from space that lands on Earth's surface; it can come from either a meteoroid or an asteroid.

**4.** Why did the asteroid explode in the atmosphere rather than smash into the ground?
There was so much heat produced when the asteroid moved through Earth's atmosphere that it caused the asteroid to explode.

**5.** Where does the Tunguska Event get its name? Place a checkmark on the correct answer below.

  The first scientist to write about the event was Dr. Ivan Tunguska.

  ✓  The asteroid exploded and destroyed a region near the Tunguska River.

  *Tunguska* is the Russian word for "asteroid."

**63**

**1.** Why was the *Dragon* spacecraft different from all previous spacecraft launched into space? The *Dragon* was the first commercial spacecraft; all previous spacecraft were built and operated by the government.

**2.** How many people usually live and work on the ISS at one time? Place a checkmark on the line of the best answer.

  2        12

  ✓ 6       25

**3.** On average, how long does a crewmember spend aboard the ISS? Place a checkmark on the line of the best answer.

  one week        six weeks

  one month      ✓ six months

**4.** What is SpaceX? Place a checkmark on the line of the best answer.

  the second commercial spacecraft to supply the ISS

  a nickname for the ISS

  ✓ the company that built the *Dragon*

  America's first space station

**5.** Write out the words represented by each acronym.
ISS: International Space Station
NASA: National Aeronautics and Space Administration
CRS: Commercial Resupply Services

**6.** Why do you think the *Dragon* capsule lands in the Pacific Ocean? Provide at least two reasons. Answers may vary. Possible answer: The capsule lands in water so the parts can be recovered; if it landed on ground, there would be more chance for damage. Also, by landing in the ocean, there is less chance of hitting buildings or people.

**7.** Provide one reason why commercial spacecraft might not be a good option for resupply missions.
Every launch and landing is extremely expensive.

**65**

**1.** Authors often have more than one purpose for writing a text. Identify two purposes for this text by placing checkmarks on the lines of the two best choices.

  ✓ entertain      ✓ inform

  convince          explain

**2.** Write a sentence that summarizes the text. Answers will vary. Possible answer: Terrence's Uncle Lance, a professional snowboarder, visits his class and explains the history of snowboarding.

**3.** A *portmanteau* is a word created by combining two or more words into a single, new word. For example, *smog* is a portmanteau word that combines *smoke* and *fog*. What two words were combined to create the portmanteau word *snurfer*?

  snow  and  surfer

**4.** Why were snowboarders banned early on from most ski resorts? Place a checkmark on the correct answer.

  Snowboards were considered unsafe to ride.

  Ski lifts were not designed to carry snowboarders up the slope.

  ✓ Snowboarders were mostly teenagers or children, and other skiers thought they were reckless.

  Snowboarders were mostly teenagers or children, and ski resorts did not believe they could afford to pay lift fees.

**5.** Why doesn't Terrence try to get Lance Nichols' autograph like the other students?
Lance is Terrence's uncle, and he will be visiting the family through the weekend, so Terrence is in no rush to get an autograph.

**6.** In your own words, explain how snowboarding is similar to riding a skateboard or a surfboard. How are they different? Answers will vary. Possible answer: Like skateboarding or surfing, snowboarding involves balancing on a flat board as it glides along. The difference is that in snowboarding, the board glides across snow and there are bindings on top that hold your feet in place. A skateboard's top surface is flat, and the board rolls on wheels. A surfboard is also flat on top, and it glides across water.

**7.** Have you ever snowboarded? If you have, what did you like or dislike about it? If you have not, would like you like to someday? Why or why not?
Answers will vary.

**67**

# Answer Key

---

**1.** Classify the following statements as **T** if a statement is true or **F** if a statement is false.

___F___ The *X* in X Games stands for *Exciting*.

___T___ For more than a decade, the X Games have been held in Los Angeles, California.

___F___ As long as an athlete is a professional in a sport featured at the X Games, he or she can be part of the competition.

___F___ The first X Games were held in Aspen, Colorado, in 1993.

___T___ From the very beginning, sports channel ESPN has played a major role in both the X Games and the Winter X Games.

___F___ In general, more people attend the Winter X Games than the X Games held each summer.

___T___ The X Games were popular right from the start.

**2.** Which event is NOT referred to in the text as a past or current X Games event? Place a checkmark on the correct answer.

___✓___ skateboard racing  _____ freestyle BMX

_____ skysurfing  _____ street luge

**3.** Why did the X Games organizers create qualifying events? What purpose do qualifying events serve?

The qualifying events were started because too many competitors wanted to participate. The qualifying events help limit the number of participants in the X Games.

**4.** The information in the text is organized in blocks of text corresponding to each year or span of years in the X Games' history. Why do you think the author chose to organize the text this way? Do you think this was or was not a good way to organize the information? Explain your answer.

Answers will vary. Possible answer: The author organized the information this way because it is somewhat like a timeline, which makes it easier to follow the history. I do not think this was a good choice, because it is boring to read. I would prefer if the history was told more like a story, with regular paragraphs.

**69**

---

**1.** Is this story fiction or nonfiction? How do you know?

The setting of Los Angeles is a real place, but the story is fiction because the characters are made up by the author.

**2.** Gabriela is excited to tell her father about finishing a "5.11b climb." Based on the context of how it is used in the story, what does 5.11b most likely refer to? Place a checkmark on the line of the best choice.

_____ cost  _____ location

___✓___ difficulty  _____ minimum age

**3.** Based on information from the text, which of the following best describes Gabriela's relationship with her father? Place a checkmark on the line of the best choice.

_____ Gabriela visits him once a year in Los Angeles.

_____ Gabriela has not seen or spoken with him in many years.

___✓___ Gabriela doesn't see her father often, but they have a good relationship.

_____ Gabriela lives with her father in Los Angeles.

**4.** Why do you think the gym requires all first-time visitors to take a basic climbing class, even if they have experience climbing at others gyms?

Answers may vary. Possible answer: The gym needs to be sure that every climber knows at least the basics, and by having new visitors take a basic course, they can be sure.

**5.** Write two words that describe Gabriela's father. Cite evidence from the story to support your choices. Answers will vary. Possible answers shown.

___artistic___ : He paints a picture of someone rock climbing

___athletic___ : He likes to rock climb.

**6.** *Lingo* is the special words used for specific activities or by those who are involved in a specific activity. Why do you think the author chose to include rock climbing lingo in the text, such as *bouldering, VB, jug,* and *flag*?

Answers may vary. Possible answer: By including lingo for rock climbing, the author makes it believable that Gabriela has experience climbing and knows how to give advice to her father.

**7.** What activities are you involved in that require special skills? Does the activity have lingo used by participants? Provide some examples of the lingo.

Answers will vary.

**71**

---

**1.** Complete the lines below by including a description of an event from Shaun White's life that corresponds to each date. Refer to the text as needed.

1986: Shaun White is born.

1990: White starts skiing.

2006: White wins his first Olympic gold medal.

2011: White wins a gold medal in skateboarding at the X Games.

2014: White failed to win a gold medal at the Winter Olympics.

**2.** Why was Shaun White nicknamed the "Flying Tomato"? He had long, red hair, and he could jump really high with a skateboard.

**3.** Shaun White has excelled at two sports in particular. What are they?

___snowboarding___  ___skateboarding___

**4.** Which of the following statements is true? Place a checkmark on the line of the correct answer.

_____ Shaun White has won gold medals at both the Summer and Winter Olympics.

_____ Shaun White has won a gold medal at each Olympics in which he competed.

___✓___ Shaun White has won gold medals at two different Winter Olympics.

_____ Shaun White has won gold medals at the Summer and Winter X Games, but not for any Olympic events.

**5.** What is Shaun White's role in the band Bad Things? Place a checkmark on the line of the correct answer.

_____ drummer  ___✓___ guitarist

_____ manager  _____ lead singer

**6.** What is the author's opinion of Shaun White? Cite evidence from the text to support your answer.

The author admires Shaun White. The author includes only positive descriptions of White and all of his accomplishments.

**7.** Do you have a favorite athlete or famous person you admire? What do you admire about this person?

Answers will vary.

**73**

# Answer Key

---

**1.** What are the two main settings in this story?

the parking lot    and    the city council chambers

**2.** What is the conflict in this story?

Skateboarders do not have a good place to skate, so they work together to try to turn a parking lot into a skate park.

**3.** How is the conflict resolved? The skateboarders work hard to convince their parents, local business owners, and the city council that the skate park is a good idea, and the plan is approved.

**4.** Authors include specific details when they write in order to make a story more interesting and believable. Identify two specific details from the story, and explain how they make the story more interesting or believable.

Answers will vary, but they should mention the names of skateboarding tricks from the story or other details that make it more believable.

**5.** A *win-win situation* is when everyone involved benefits from results. How is the building of the skate park an example of a win-win situation?

The skate park will benefit the skateboarders because it will give them a safe, fun place to go skateboarding. The park will also benefit the store owners, because the skaters will be less likely to skateboard in front of their businesses.

**6.** If the other skaters had chosen not to help, do you think Sophia and Braxton would have succeeded with the skate park plan? Explain your answer.

Answers will vary. Possible answer: No, they would not have succeeded. With just the two of them, they would not have been able to contact anywhere near as many parents or business owners. Without their support at the council meeting, the plans would most likely not be approved.

**7.** Describe a time when you were part of group working toward a common goal. What was your role? Would the goal have been achieved without everyone's help?

Answers will vary.

**75**

---

**1.** Where did the Baltimore & Ohio Railroad get its name? Place a checkmark on the line of the correct answer.

_____ The railroad was founded by businessmen from Baltimore and Ohio.

_____ The first steam engines were manufactured in Baltimore and Ohio.

✓ The railroad ran from Baltimore to the Ohio River.

_____ The railroad was found by Charles Baltimore and Nicholas Ohio.

**2.** Why was Baltimore considered a good location to start a railroad company?

Baltimore was a major seaport, and it was located farther inland than any of the other seaports.

**3.** Complete the sentence below.

"Tom Thumb" was the nickname of America's first steam locomotive.

**4.** Describe the impact of the Civil War on the B&O Railroad.

During the Civil War, the railroad was often attacked by Confederate soldiers. They damaged the railroad, and costly repairs had to be made after the war.

**5.** Even though steam engines were available when the B&O Railroad began operating, the first trains were pulled by horses. Why?

At first, the horse-drawn trains were able to travel faster than the earliest steam locomotive.

**6.** Place checkmark on the line of the answer that best completes the sentence.

The 19th century refers to the _____

_____ 1700s          _____ 1900s

✓ 1800s          _____ 2000s

**7.** The author writes that steam locomotives were the main source of long-distance travel in the 1800s. What mode of transportation do you think became the main source of long-distance travel in the 1900s? Explain your answer.

Answers will vary, but students should describe how either automobiles or airplanes took over the role of railroads as the main source of long-distance transportation.

**77**

---

**1.** Which of the following best describes Jeremiah's relationship with Grandpa Watkins? Place a checkmark on the line of the best answer.

_____ Jeremiah is meeting his grandfather for the first time.

✓ Jeremiah has met his grandfather a few times in the past, but they don't know each other very well.

_____ Jeremiah and his grandfather have a very close relationship and spend a lot of time together.

_____ Jeremiah lives with Grandpa and Grandma Watkins.

**2.** Who else from Jeremiah's family has come along for the visit to his grandparent's home? Place a checkmark on the correct answer.

_____ his mother and father          _____ his mother, sister, and brother

_____ his mother, father, sister, and brother          ✓ The story does not say.

**3.** Why is Jeremiah surprised when Grandpa Watkins turns on the lights?

He imagined a much smaller model train set, similar to something he might have had when he was little.

**4.** What do you think impressed Jeremiah the most about the model train set? Explain your answer. Answers may vary. Possible answer: Jeremiah is most impressed with the amount of work and skill that it took to build the model. The author describes how Jeremiah's first reaction is to understand how much work was involved. Then, before he even thinks about running the trains, he walks around the model and admires it.

**5.** Why does Jeremiah feel uncomfortable during breakfast? Do you think he feels the same way at the end of the story? Explain your answer.

Answers may vary. Possible answer: Jeremiah is uncomfortable at breakfast because he doesn't know how he should act around his grandparents. I don't think he feels the same way at the end, because he has had a chance to get to know Grandpa Watkins better while they play with the train set.

**6.** Make a prediction about the future of Jeremiah's relationship with his grandfather.

Answers will vary. Possible answer: I think Jeremiah and Grandpa Watkins will have a good relationship, because they got to know each other better during the visit. Also, Grandpa Watkins' goofy grin hints that he may have a similar personality to Jeremiah, who is also described as liking to goof around.

**79**

---

# Answer Key

---

**1.** Which of the following best describes the theme of the John Henry tale? Place a checkmark on the line of the best answer choice.

   ✓    A human being's desire to work hard and succeed is stronger than a machine.

_____ Someday, all human labor will be replaced by machines, and it is a losing battle to fight against this fact.

_____ The owners of railroad companies wanted to see progress, no matter what the cost.

_____ Each of us succeeds or fails on our own, and others will seldom step forward to help.

**2.** Who is the protagonist in the story? ___John Henry___

**3.** Who is the antagonist in the story? ___the drilling machine___

**4.** What is the conflict in the story? ___John Henry must beat the drilling machine in a race to prove that he is stronger, and therefore has more value, than the machine.___

**5.** Which part of the story is the climax? Place a checkmark on the line of the correct answer.

_____ when John Henry dies       _____ when John Henry accepts the challenge to race

   ✓    when John Henry wins the race      _____ when the machine arrives

**6.** Is this a realistic story or a fantasy? Explain your answer.

___Answers will vary. Possible answer: This story is a fantasy, because a human being wouldn't really be able to beat the drilling machine.___

**7.** Imagine a retelling of this story as if it took place now. How would it be different? What would the machine be? What job would the John Henry character have? Would the outcome be the same? Describe what you imagine on the lines below.

___Answers will vary.___

_____

_____

_____

**81**

---

**1.** Draw a line from each band member's first name to his last name.

John          Harrison

Paul          Starr

George        McCartney

Ringo         Lennon

**2.** Write a sentence to summarize each paragraph of the text.

1. ___John Lennon formed the Quarrymen to play rock and roll.___
2. ___Paul McCartney and George Harrison join the band, and they become the Beatles.___
3. ___The Beatles become popular in Liverpool, and travel to Germany to play, also.___
4. ___Brian Epstein becomes The Beatles manager.___
5. ___Ringo Starr joins the band, and they record their first single.___
6. ___The Beatles become wildly popular in England, and Beatlemania is born.___
7. ___The Beatles travel to America, where they are equally popular.___
8. ___The Beatles become the most popular band of the 1960s.___

**3.** Classify the following statements as **T** if a statement is true or **F** if a statement is false.

___F___ The Silver Beetles first formed in Hamburg, Germany, in the late-1950s.

___T___ John Lennon loved American rock and roll music.

___T___ Ringo Starr's real name is Richard Starkey.

___F___ Beatlemania was born when The Beatles toured America in 1964.

___F___ Before joining the Beatles, Paul McCartney had his own band called The Quarrymen.

___T___ The Beatles manager got them to wear matching suits when they played.

**4.** If The Beatles were a band today, how would their story be different? How would it be the same? Be specific.

___Answers will vary, but should include ideas about how technology, including the Internet, has changed the way artists/bands become popular, as well as what kinds of music are most popular today.___

**83**

---

As indicated, provide either a cause or an effect to complete each cause-and-effect relationship below. Answers may vary. Possible answers shown. you provide must make

**1. cause:** ___Cameron played his electric guitar.___

    **effect:** A loud *kerrrrang!* sound came from the garage.

**2. cause:** ___Mackenzie learned that the band would be performing in front of an audience.___

    **effect:** Mackenzie's stomach started doing flip-flops again.

**3. cause:** Mackenzie did not recognize the title of the song the band was playing.

    **effect:** ___Cameron sang for the first two times the band played the song.___

**4. cause:** Cameron knew Mackenzie was a good singer.

    **effect:** ___Cameron invited Mackenzie to sing with the band.___

**5.** Provide your own example of a cause-and-effect relationship from the story.

    **cause:** ___Answers will vary.___

    **effect:** _____

**6.** What four instruments are played in the band?

___guitar___    ___bass___    ___keyboard___    ___drums___

**7.** What inspired Cameron to name the band *The Racket*?

___His grandmother said they made a racket when they played.___

**8.** Mackenzie has been singing for years, so why is she nervous about singing with the band?

___She has never sang alone before, it has always been as part of a chorus.___

**9.** Why does Mackenzie stop feeling nervous during practice? ___She is trying hard to sing well, so it takes her mind off of feeling nervous.___

**10.** Why is Mackenzie surprised to discover that Grayson is in the band? ___Grayson is a very quiet person, and she did not expect him to be in a band.___

**11.** If you formed a band, what would you call it? Why?

___Answers will vary.___

_____

_____

**85**

---

Spectrum Reading Grade 7

Answer Key

**144**

# Answer Key

**1.** Which of the following types of music is LEAST likely to use an electric guitar? Place a checkmark on the line of the best answer.

_____ blues      _____ country

_____ jazz      ✓ classical

**2.** Which of the following instruments was NOT mentioned in the text as being an ancestor of the guitar? Place a checkmark on the line of the correct answer.

✓ lyre      _____ harp

_____ lute      _____ fiddle

**3.** How does the author organize the text? Place a checkmark on the line of the best answer.

_____ comparing and contrasting      _____ cause and effect

✓ time order      _____ subject

**4.** Who was "Lucille"?

Lucille was B. B. King's guitar.

**5.** How were Jimi Hendrix's guitars different from most other guitars?

He strung his guitars backward so he could play them left-handed.

**6.** A guitar's neck forms the fingerboard. When a string is pressed against the fingerboard, it shortens the part of the string that will vibrate when it is plucked. Why is this important?

Changing the length of the part of the string that vibrates changes the note produced by the vibrations.

**7.** What was the main reason for inventing guitars that were electric?

amplification, or making them louder

**8.** Do you play an instrument? If so, which instrument, and why did you choose it? If not, is there an instrument you would like to learn how to play? Why?

Answers will vary.

**87**

---

**1.** Write a one-sentence summary of the story. Mackenzie is nervous about performing in front of a huge audience, but her hard work and practice make the performance easy, and she ends up having fun.

**2.** Which of the following does NOT describe one of the story's themes? Place a checkmark on the line of the best answer.

_____ Trying new things, even if they make you nervous, can be rewarding.

_____ People often have unexpected talents.

✓ A bit of luck can lead to unexpected rewards.

_____ With hard work, you can achieve great things.

**3.** How was the song "Let's Make a Racket!" different from the other two songs the band played?

It was an original written by Grayson.

**4.** Why do you think it helped Mackenzie's nervousness that she couldn't see the audience very well? The audience was less intimidating because she couldn't see all the faces.

**5.** Which of the following was NOT a song played by The Racket? Place a checkmark on the line of the correct answer.

✓ "Wild Thing"      _____ "Let's Make a Racket!"

_____ "Louie, Louie"      _____ "I Wanna Hold Your Hand"

**6.** Despite being scared, Mackenzie went onstage and preformed anyway. What does this tell you about her character?

She is brave, and she would not let down her bandmates.

**7.** Why was Grayson's performance in particular a surprise to the audience?

Everyone saw him as being shy, but he performed a wild drum solo on stage in front of the whole school.

**8.** Why wasn't Mackenzie worried about whether or not the band would win a prize?

Finding out that she had the confidence to perform in front of a huge audience was enough of a reward for her.

**9.** Have you ever met someone who later surprised you by having a talent or an aspect of his or her personality that you didn't expect? Explain what it was that surprised you and why it was surprising.

Answers will vary.

**89**

---

**1.** Classify the following statements as **T** if a statement is true or **F** if a statement is false.

F The Westminster Dog Show is the longest-running sporting event the United States.

T All of the dogs competing in the Westminster Dog Show have already won honors in other dog shows.

F Dogs race through agility courses as one part of the Westminster Dog Show competition.

F A ticket to the show is the only way to view the competition.

T Throughout its 100+ years, many famous celebrities have attended the Westminster Dog Show.

F The way a dog looks is the only factor used to determine whether or not it will win top honors for its breed.

**2.** What does AKC stand for? Place a checkmark on the line of the correct answer.

_____ Associated Kennel Competition      ✓ American Kennel Club

_____ American Kennel Canines      _____ Association of Kindness to Canines

**3.** On the line following each date, write a short sentence describing the important event from that year described in the text.

1877: This was the first year the competition was held.

1905: By this year, Westminster had become the biggest dog show in the world.

1918: In this year, the dog show donated its profits to help during World War I.

2006: In this year, the dog show donated profits to help Gulf Coast residents.

2014: A fox terrier named Sadie won the 2014 Westminster Dog Show.

**4.** Does the author believe the Westminster Dog Show is good for dogs or not good for dogs? Support your answer with evidence from the text.

Answers will vary. Possible answer: The author believes the dog show is good for dogs. The author describes many of the dog show's positive aspects, such as donating money to causes. The author also uses many positive words to describe the event, such as *success* and *popularity*.

**5.** Describe your own pet(s), or a pet you would like to have.

Answers will vary.

**91**

# Answer Key

**1.** Who is the main character in the story? Lorenzo

**2.** What is the setting? an auditorium used for dog agility classes

**3.** What breed of dog is Mia? mostly collie

**4.** What are the characteristics of the breed, and why did Lorenzo think they would be a good match for the family?
Collies are smart and friendly, and since Lorenzo has young siblings, a friendly dog was a good match.

**5.** Do you think Mia will succeed at agility? Support your answer with evidence from the text. Answers will vary. Possible answer: Mia will succeed at agility. Lorenzo is described as having a strong bond with Mia, so that will help. Lorenzo has also already gotten Mia to jump through a tire at the park. This shows his dedication, as well as her ability to perform the kinds of activities in agility.

**6.** If a reader does not know the meaning of the word *equestrian*, what context clue does the author provide to help clarify the meaning?
After saying they had attended an equestrian event, the author has Mrs. Martinez say, "My cousin likes to ride horses," which helps clarify that people ride horses at an equestrian event.

**7.** Which of the following is NOT a piece of dog agility equipment described in the story? Place a checkmark on the line of the correct answer.
\_\_\_\_\_ A-frame ramp          \_\_\_\_\_ dogwalk
\_\_\_\_\_ suspended tire          ✓ tunnel

**8.** Think of a human sports and physical competition. Which one do you think is the best comparison to dog agility? Write the sport you chose, and then explain your answer.
Answers will vary.

**93**

**1.** According to the text, what was Cesar Millan's dream? Place a checkmark on the line of the correct answer.
\_\_\_\_\_ to have his own TV show          ✓ to be the best dog trainer in the world
\_\_\_\_\_ to train dogs in Hollywood          \_\_\_\_\_ to have his own website

**2.** Who was Daddy? Place a checkmark on the line of the correct answer.
\_\_\_\_\_ Cesar's grandfather          \_\_\_\_\_ Jada Pinkett-Smith's dog
✓ Cesar's pit bull          \_\_\_\_\_ the first dog Cesar trained

**3.** What was the name of Cesar Millan's TV show? The Dog Whisperer

**4.** Is this text an autobiography or biography? Explain your answer.
The text is a biography because the author is telling about someone else's life. An autobiography is when the author tells about his or her own life.

**5.** What actions did Cesar Millan take to work toward his success? Provide three examples.
Cesar moved to the United States. He worked for free at first to share his talents. He opened his own business.

**6.** Provide three examples of how others helped Cesar Millan achieve his success.
Cesar's grandfather taught him some things about dog behavior. Jada Pinkett-Smith paid to help him learn English. TV producers helped him get a television show.

**7.** How does the author organize the text? Place a checkmark on the line of the best answer.
\_\_\_\_\_ grouping similar ideas          \_\_\_\_\_ describing the steps of a process
✓ time order          \_\_\_\_\_ comparing and contrasting

**8.** The author describes how Cesar watched the way his dog reacted to each producer in order to decide which producer to choose. How do you think the dog reacted when he didn't like someone? How did the dog react when he did like someone?
Answers will vary.

**95**

**1.** In which state does the Iditarod take place? Place a checkmark on the line of the correct answer.
\_\_\_\_\_ Washington          \_\_\_\_\_ Montana
\_\_\_\_\_ North Dakota          ✓ Alaska

**2.** Which of the following is a reasonable estimate for how long the Iditarod race lasts? Place a checkmark on the line of the best answer.
\_\_\_\_\_ 2 days          \_\_\_\_\_ 2 weeks
✓ 8 days          \_\_\_\_\_ 1 month

**3.** Describe how Jo helps her family prepare for the Iditarod.
Early in the morning and at night, Jo helps take care of the dogs by making sure they have food and water.

**4.** Explain why the Iditarod starts twice. The first start is just an unofficial ceremony in Anchorage. The second start is the official start of the race, and it happens in a different city.

**5.** Which of the following statements describes why the Smiths compete in the Iditarod each year? Place a checkmark on the line of the best answer.
\_\_\_\_\_ The winner of the Iditarod receives a large cash reward, and the Smiths hope that winning the money could change their lives.
✓ Racing in the Iditarod is a family tradition that has been passed down for a few generations.
\_\_\_\_\_ The Smiths raise sled dogs, and having their dogs race in the Iditarod means that the dogs will be worth a lot more money.
\_\_\_\_\_ Everyone who lives in their area is required to take part in the race as a form of emergency training in case of severe weather.

**6.** What is the significance of the red light at the race's finish line?
The red light stays on until all the dog sled teams have arrived safely at the finish line.

**7.** Why does each dog have a microchip implanted under its skin?
The microchips allow the race organizers to track where the dogs and the riders are located along the race trail.

**8.** What chores or other tasks do you do to help your family?
Answers will vary.

**97**

# Answer Key

**1.** Write a sentence that summarizes the story. Answers will vary. Possible answer: When a family needs to replace their old car, they discuss the benefits of owning a hybrid.

**2.** What is the author's main purpose for writing the story? Place a checkmark on the line of the best answer.

_____ to tell an entertaining story about a family who needs to replace their old car

✓ to describe the benefits of owning a hybrid automobile

_____ to describe problems associated with owning a hybrid automobile

_____ to describe the inconvenience of auto emissions tests

**3.** What makes a hybrid automobile different from traditional automobiles?
A hybrid automobile uses both gasoline and electricity as fuel sources. A traditional automobile uses only gasoline.

**4.** Write a sentence describing the author's point of view about hybrid automobiles.
The author thinks hybrid automobiles are a better choice than traditional automobiles.

**5.** Does the author support his or her point of view with sufficient evidence and sound reasoning? Cite examples from the text in your answer.
Answers may vary. Possible answer: Yes, the author supports his/her point of view with evidence. The author describes many benefits to owning a hybrid, such as fuel efficiency and little to no pollution. When one drawback is mentioned (few recharging stations), the author explains why this is only a minor drawback, especially compared to the benefits.

**6.** If this story took place 50 years ago, how would it be different? What elements might be the same? Answers will vary. Possible answer: The family would not be discussing hybrid vehicles, because they did not exist 50 years ago. However, they might still be discussing what kind of car to get, as well as the benefits of saving money.

**7.** Hybrid automobiles are one way to use fewer fossil fuels and reduce pollution. Name two others. Answers will vary. Possible answers:
riding a bike    using public transportation

**99**

---

**1.** Write a sentence t[hat] Answers will vary. Possible answers:
1. The World Solar Challenge is a race of solar-powered vehicles held every other year in Australia.
2. Competitors come from all over the world.
3. Each vehicle must meet a set of guidelines in order to compete.
4. The cars must get nearly all of their power from the sun.
5. Teams must rely on themselves to complete the race, which usually lasts for nearly two straight days.

**2.** Participants from which of the following nations have had the most success at the World Solar Challenge? Place a checkmark on the line of the best answer.

_____ the United States       _____ China

✓ the Netherlands       _____ Australia

**3.** List two of the requirements that vehicles must meet in order to compete in the World Solar Challenge. Answers will vary. Possible answers:
Solar panels can be no more than six square meters in size. Cars can store no more than 5 kilowatt hours of power.

**4.** Why do you think the speeds and distances in the text are described in terms of kilometers rather than miles? Answers may vary. Possible answer: Most of the world uses metric measurements. Since this is an international competition, the measurements are described using the metric system.

**5.** Complete the sentence below.
Each vehicle in the World Solar Challenge weighs about as much as a refrigerator.

**6.** What do the winners of the WSC usually do as part of the celebration?
jump into a fountain

**7.** Other than entertainment, what do you think is a benefit that comes from having a race like the World Solar Challenge? Answers may vary. Possible answer:
The challenge of building an efficient and reliable solar-powered vehicle can help lead to solar-powered cars being used someday by regular people.

**8.** Imagine if all of the vehicles where you live were solar-powered. Describe how your town or city would be different than it is now with mostly gas-powered vehicles.
Answers will vary.

**101**

---

**1.** Why is the story titled *Galaxie Guys*?
The two main characters are working together to restore an old car called a Galaxie.

**2.** Why are Sebastian and his dad going to an auto salvage lot?
They are looking for a grille for the Ford Galaxie they are restoring.

**3.** Authors include sensory details to make their stories more interesting. Sensory details describe sights, sounds, smells, tastes, and textures experienced by the characters. Which two senses does the author provide details for in the story? Provide two examples for each sense.

Sense: sight

Example 1: description of warehouses and abandoned factories

Example 2: description of the various cars at the salvage yard

Sense: sound

Example 1: classical music in the car

Example 2: bluegrass music in the car

**4.** Did Sebastian enjoy the trip to the auto salvage yard? How do you know?
Yes. The author describes how much he appreciates all the old cars at the salvage yard, and he says, "That place was really cool," as they leave the lot.

**5.** What kind of relationship does Sebastian have with his dad? Support your answer with evidence from the text. Answers may vary. Possible answer: He and his dad have a companionable relationship. They spend time together working on the car, and they have fun listening to each other's music.

**6.** Sebastian usually plays classical music in the car when it's his turn to choose. What do your think influenced his choice of a bluegrass station at the end of the story?
Answers may vary. Possible answer: When Sebastian is at the salvage yard, he recognizes how much he likes the variety in all the different cars he sees. He might have decided that some variety in the music he likes would be just as enjoyable, so he chose a new station.

**7.** When you get to choose music to play in the car, what do you choose? Why?
Answers will vary.

**103**

# Answer Key

---

**105**

1. List three mc **Answers may vary. Possible answers:**
   Japanese Americans were unjustly detained in camps during World War II.
   Japan's attack on Pearl Harbor led to a wave of anti-Japanese feelings in the U.S.
   The camps became like small villages, with businesses and sports teams.

2. Choose one of the ideas you wrote above, and identify details or evidence from the text that support the idea. **Answers will vary. Possible answer: The author**
   describes how innocent Americans were placed in the camps only
   because they were of Japanese descent. Even children were shipped
   away, which is really unjust. Also, the camps were ended because the
   Supreme Court ruled that they were unjust.

3. Why were detained Japanese Americans finally allowed to return home? Place a checkmark on the line of the correct answer.

   _____ The United States defeated Japan, and World War II ended.

   _____ President Roosevelt declared the camps unjust, and he ordered the release of all detainees.

   __✓__ The Supreme Court ruled that it was against the law to detain American citizens without just cause.

   _____ The American people insisted that the camps were unjust, so their representatives in the U.S. Congress voted to close the camps and release the detainees.

4. Analyze the way *infamy* is used in the first and final sentences of the text. Which of the following best describes the meaning of *infamy*? Place a checkmark on the line of the best answer.

   _____ an event that is unjust          _____ remembered for a long time

   __✓__ a negative kind of fame          _____ a violent act during wartime

5. What did the detainees do to make life more bearable in the camps? Why do think these actions were important?
   Answers may vary. Possible answer: They decorated their
   barracks, and they planted flowers and other plants around the
   camp. They also opened businesses and formed sports teams.
   These actions were important because it helped them feel less
   defeated or depressed while have to endure an unfair situation.

---

**107**

1. Who is the protagonist, or main character, in the story?
   The protagonist is Araki.

2. The antagonist of a story is the opponent or enemy that the protagonist must struggle against. Identify the antagonist in this story. The antagonist in this story is not
   a person; it is the fact that the family is being evacuated unfairly.

3. Do you think Araki defeats the antagonist? Why or why not? Cite evidence from the story in your answer. Answers may vary. Possible answer: Yes, Araki defeats
   the antagonist because he does not let the awful circumstances
   defeat his good nature. He may be scared and even angry, but at the
   end, he is trying hard to look at the situation as an adventure.

4. Why does Mr. Yamamoto think running away is a bad idea? He has heard that those
   who try to run away and are caught get sent to camps that are like
   prisons.

5. Read or review the previous story, *Internment During WWII*. It is a nonfiction historical text about the same event affecting the fictional Yamamotos in this story. Compare and contrast the two texts. Which do you think is a more effective way to tell about history? Explain your answer.
   Answers may vary. Possible answer: The nonfiction text includes lots
   of dates and descriptions of real events that happened. It discusses
   the Japanese American detainees as a whole group, and does not
   focus on anyone specifically. The events in the story are based on
   true events, but the specific characters are made up. I think the
   fiction story has more impact, because I can relate more to what is
   happening to these specific people. It makes the events seem more
   real. The fact-based, historical account contains more information
   about the event, but it makes the event seem distant and long-ago.

6. Based on what you have read in this story and the previous nonfiction text, make a prediction about Araki's experiences at the relocation camp. Support your prediction with evidence from the texts.
   Araki will try to make the best of the situation. The
   nonfiction text says that many of those in the camps tried
   to do that as well. At the end of the story, Araki is already
   trying to find some kind of positive way to live through the
   experience.

---

**109**

1. Write a few sentences summarizing the story.
   Answers may vary. Possible answer: Lila visits her grandparents to
   interview them about their lives. She is surprised to learn that they
   had been part of the relocation of Japanese Americans during World
   War II. Grandpa Yamamoto describes his experiences at the camp,
   and Lila learns that the camp is where her grandparents first met.

2. Why does Grandpa Araki say the camp was "like a little-village"?
   The people at the camps started small businesses, and most of the same
   kinds of social interactions happened at the camps as in any community.

3. How would the story be different if Grandpa Araki had spent his life angry and bitter about his experiences at the camp? Answers will vary. Possible answer: Grandpa Araki
   might describe how awful the camps were. He would focus on the Supreme Court's
   decision that the camps were unjust. Instead, he would focus on how unfair things are and
   how angry he was about the actions of non-Japanese Americans.

4. Why does Grandpa Araki say he "never lost faith in America," despite his family's unjust detention? Grandpa Araki believes that United States may not
   be perfect, but its laws and the structure of government
   are in place to right the wrongs that might happen.

5. Which of the following best describes Lila's reason for visiting her grandparents? Place a checkmark on the line of the best answer.

   _____ When Lila found out that her grandparents had lived at one of the relocation camps, she wanted to learn more about their experiences.

   __✓__ As part of a school assignment, Lila wanted to interview her grandparents about their lives.

   _____ Lila was writing a school report about the relocation camps, and she wanted to get a first-hand account of her grandparents' experiences.

   _____ Lila was at her grandparents' house for a holiday visit.

6. What were two positive events for her grandparents that occurred at the camp?
   Grandpa Araki learned to play baseball, and he and
   Grandma Mai met there.

7. Have you ever had something positive happen as a result of an otherwise negative event? Describe what happened, or describe an imaginary scenario in which a negative event has some kind of positive aspect to it.
   Answers will vary.

# Answer Key

---

**Page 111**

1. How is the text organized? Place a checkmark on the line of the best answer.

   _____ time order      ✓ steps of a process

   _____ comparing and contrasting      _____ similar ideas

2. What is *genealogy*?

   the study of a family's history

3. What occupation does the author compare someone studying genealogy to?

   detective

4. Which of the following best summarizes the author's point of view about genealogical research? Place a checkmark on the line of the best answer.

   ✓ Researching your family's genealogy can be a lot of work, but the work is rewarding.

   _____ The easiest way to research your family's genealogy is to use an Internet family tree search service.

   _____ Public record databases contain many errors and gaps in information, so they should mostly be avoided.

   _____ You must take notes when you are researching your family's genealogy, otherwise you will have to work twice as hard.

5. What is the author's advice if you follow a path back through your family's history, but the path turns out to be wrong?

   Do not get discouraged. Back up to where you know the facts are right, and start again.

6. List three places mentioned in the text where someone can look for information about their family's history. Answers will vary. Possible answers:

   obituaries      newspapers      military records

7. According to the text, what is the first step you should take if you want information about your family's history?

   Talk to your older relatives to find out what they know

8. Write a short paragraph describing what you know about your family's history, such as where your ancestors lived, what your grandparents did for a living, and so on.

   Answers will vary.

**111**

---

**Page 113**

1. What is the main idea of this story? How does the author develop this idea? Cite evidence from the story in your answer. Answers may vary. Possible answer: The main idea is that a bluegrass festival is a fun place to visit. The author develops this idea by having the main character enjoy himself at the festival. For example, Charley get to eat funnel cake, he loves watching the man play spoons, and he is pleasantly surprised to hear an electric bluegrass band.

2. Why do you think Charley wants to pretend he is at the festival by himself?

   Answers will vary. Possible answer: Charley wants to imagine himself as more of a grown-up, and not a kid who has to be there with his parents.

3. Which of the following instruments is NOT mentioned at some point in the story? Place a checkmark on the line of the correct answer.

   _____ harmonica      ✓ ukulele

   _____ banjo      _____ mandolin

4. Authors include sensory details to make their stories more interesting. Sensory details describe sights, sounds, smells, tastes, and textures experienced by the characters. Find examples in the text Answers will vary. Possible answers: _____ ses and examples below.

   Sense: taste      Example: sweet, chewy bite of funnel cake

   Sense: sight      Example: speakers on either side of the stage; white beard

   Sense: smell      Example: slightly sweet, meaty smell near the food vendors

5. How do Charley's feelings about bluegrass music change by the end of the story? Why do they change? At first, Charley thinks all bluegrass music sounds the same. At the end of the story, he realizes this is not true. The change happened because he heard his uncle's electric bluegrass band, which was a style he had never heard before.

6. How would this story be different if it were told from Uncle Vernon's perspective? Give at least two examples.

   Answers will vary. Possible answer: If the story were told from Uncle Vernon's viewpoint, the story would include descriptions of what it is like backstage. It might also include scenes with some of the other band members or musicians performing at the festival.

7. Compare and contrast the festival in the story to a fair, festival, or other event you have attended. Describe at least two ways they are similar and two ways they are different.

   Answers will vary.

**113**

---

**Page 115**

1. Classify the following statements by writing **O** if the statement is an opinion, or **F** if the statement is a fact.

   F  Carrie Underwood's number-one hit "Inside Your Heaven" was also the best-selling single of the year.

   O  Carrie Underwood's success was largely based on the luck of winning *American Idol*, and only in small part due to her talent.

   O  Her album *Some Hearts* was the best country release of 2006.

   F  Immediately after high school, Carrie Underwood chose to attend college rather than continue pursuing a career in music.

   F  The people at Capitol Records wanted to make a record with Carrie Underwood, but circumstances changed, and the record was never made.

   F  Viewers of *American Idol*'s fourth season chose Carrie Underwood as their favorite singer.

   F  Checotah, Oklahoma, is a rural town in the eastern part of the state.

   F  In 2007, Carrie Underwood won a Grammy Award for Best New Artist.

2. Why does the author say that Carrie Underwood's *American Idol* win "changed her life forever"? If it wasn't for her win on *American Idol*, she would not have received the recording contract, and her career may have turned out very different.

3. Identify three main ideas from the text. Write them on the lines below.

   Answers may vary. Possible answers: Carrie Underwood is a very talented singer. Because of her win on *American Idol*, she was able to launch a successful recording career. Carrie Underwood is very wealthy, but she donates some of her wealth to help others.

4. Choose an adjective that describes Carrie Underwood, and explain why you chose it.

   Answers will vary.

5. Popular singers and other kinds of entertainers can make a tremendous amount of money. Do you think they deserve that much wealth? Why or why not?

   Answers will vary.

**115**

---

# Answer Key

## Page 117

1. Write a one-sentence summary of the text. Answers will vary. Possible answer: After the Morrisons move to Nashville, they spend a week visiting a few of the city's musical landmarks.

2. Identify two purposes the author had for writing the story.
to entertain; to inform

3. List three facts from the story.
Elvis record at RCA Studio B. The Grand Ole Opry started as a radio show in an office building. The Country Music Hall of Fame has cars on display.

4. Choose two characters from the story, and identify what each loved seeing most.
Character: Mr. Morrison     Favorite thing: RCA Studio B
Character: Samantha     Favorite thing: Country Music Hall of Fame

5. Why were the Morrisons in Nashville? Place a checkmark on the line of the correct answer.
_____ The Morrisons took a vacation to visit the Grand Ole Opry and other sites in the city.
_____ Samantha Morrison was moving to Nashville to attend college.
✓ The family moved to Nashville because Mr. Morrison was starting a new job located there.
_____ The family was visiting Mrs. Morrison's relatives who lived in Nashville.

6. What is special about the circle onstage at the Grand Ole Opry?
The circle was cut from the Ryman Auditorium stage, which was the original home of the Grand Ole Opry.

7. Why were the Grand Ole Opry performances moved back to the Ryman Auditorium temporarily in recent years? Nashville experienced flooding that damaged the current home of the Grand Ole Opry.

8. Why do you think cultural landmarks are preserved? Are they as important as historical landmarks, such as battlefields or the birthplaces of political leaders? Explain your answer.
Answers will vary.

**117**

## Page 119

1. What is the meaning of the Japanese word *tsunami*? Place a checkmark on the line of the correct answer.
_____ wave destruction          _____ giant wave
_____ trench wave          ✓ harbor wave

2. What causes a tsunami? Place a checkmark on the line of the correct answer.
_____ hurricane          _____ monsoon
✓ earthquake          _____ typhoon

3. What happens along a coastline just prior to the arrival of a tsunami?
The ocean water recedes.

4. What natural feature helped protect the island of Maldives when the 2004 tsunami washed over the island?
coral reef

5. What are *aftershocks*?
smaller earthquakes that commonly occur after the mainshock

6. Complete the following sentences.
The *crest* of a wave is the _____ top _____ part.
The *trough* of a wave is the _____ bottom _____ part.

7. How are nations working together to help protect each other from future tsunamis?
Many nations in the Pacific Ocean's Ring of Fire have monitoring stations that measure small changes in air pressure or sea level. They can then alert other nations as early as possible to any threat of a tsunami.

8. The word *seismic* refers to events related to _____.
Place a checkmark on the line of the word that best completes the above sentence.
_____ tsunamis          ✓ earthquakes
_____ wave          _____ nuclear reactors

9. How could you help those who have been affected by tsunamis?
Answers will vary.

**119**

## Page 121

1. What details does the author include to show how angry Jayden is?
The author shows Jayden kicking the ball hard against the wall. He wants to hear it making a lot of noise.

2. What does Jayden do that helps him calm down?
He lies down on his bed for a while.

3. Which of the following statements best describes the arrangement Mr. Reynolds has made with the cleanup company he will work for in Japan?
_____ Mr. Reynolds will earn a large salary and have all expenses paid while they are in Japan.
✓ Mr. Reynolds will earn a small income, and he and the family will live rent free in an apartment.
_____ Mr. Reynolds will work as a volunteer and earn no income while they are in Japan.
_____ Mr. Reynolds will pay a fee to be allowed to move to Japan and help with the clean up.

4. What does Mr. Reynolds' reaction to the disaster tell you about his character?
Mr. Reynolds is a caring and generous person. His immediate reaction is to figure out a way he can use his skills and knowledge to help the people who were affected by the tsunami.

5. Compare Jayden's feelings about the move at the beginning of the story with his feelings at the end. Cite examples from the text to support your answer.
Answers may vary. Possible answer: At the beginning of the story, Jayden is very angry about the move and thinking only about how the tsunami has affected his life. By the end of the story, he realizes that the tsunami has been much more devastating to others, and he decides the move won't be that bad.

6. Why did Jayden's feelings change?
Answers may vary. Possible answer: He saw photos of the devastation, including one with kids his age on a soccer field. He plays soccer, so he could relate to the kids, and it made him understand better how tough it must be for them.

7. How do you react to feelings of anger? Describe any techniques you have found that help you deal with anger.
Answers will vary.

**121**

# Answer Key

---

**1.** Which of the following is NOT described as an effect of the earthquake? Place a checkmark on the line of the correct answer.

✓ windows rattling     _____ car alarms squawking

_____ vases breaking     _____ their mother phoning

**2.** Why do you think Kayla feels nauseous after the earthquake?

Answers may vary. Possible answer: The moving ground made her feel a little sick, like you might feel if you are seasick or carsick.

**3.** The author does not state that the earthquake occurred on a school day. How do you know that it did?

The author describes Christopher as eating his "afterschool snack." Kayla is described as having gotten home already from school and is doing her homework.

**4.** What was the first sign that an earthquake was occurring?

Christopher sees the milk in the bowl trembling.

**5.** Why does Christopher peak at his sister when they are under the table?

He wants to see how Kayla is reacting, partly to reassure himself that he isn't overreacting, but also to ensure that his sister won't lie later on about being unafraid.

**6.** Cite evidence from the story to describe how the siblings feel about each other.

The siblings are shown teasing each other, but that's what most siblings do. They care about each other, because after the earthquake they immediately ask how each other are doing.

**7.** Write a sentence to summarize the story. Answers will vary. Possible answer: A brother and sister experience the scare of an earthquake, but soon afterward life is back to normal as they tease each other.

**8.** Why are Christopher and his mother fine with the fact that several objects broke during the earthquake?

A few broken objects can be replaced, and that's much better than if someone had been seriously injured.

**9.** Do you think hiding under the table was good decision? Why or why not?

Answers will vary.

**123**

---

**1.** The greatest danger to human life during an earthquake is _____

Place a checkmark on the line of the word or phrase that best completes the sentence.

_____ seismic waves     ✓ damaged or collapsing structures

_____ damage to Earth's crust     _____ retrofitted bridges and buildings

**2.** Which of the following best describes the text's central idea? Place a checkmark on the line of the best answer.

_____ Earthquakes cause widespread damage to urban areas, where buildings and other structures are at risk of collapsing.

_____ Retrofitting older buildings increases the chance that they will remain standing and undamaged during an earthquake.

✓ Using instruments to study how buildings react to earthquakes, researchers are developing safer building methods and retrofitting older structures.

_____ Scientists are studying ancient structures that have withstood centuries of earthquakes to help them understand how to build safer modern structures.

**3.** Review the text for the meanings of the following words. Write a definition in your own words for each one.

crust: Earth's outermost layer

building codes: rules that show how things must be built

retrofit: to add on afterward

footings: the part of a bridge that attaches to the ground

**4.** Why have some ancient structures survived numerous earthquakes? Why are buildings today not built in the same way? Some ancient structures were massive and build of heavy stone, so earthquakes did not damage them. Today, it would be too expensive and impractical to make those kinds of buildings.

**5.** How is the text organized? Place a checkmark on the line of the best answer.

_____ time order     _____ comparing and contrasting

_____ pros and cons     ✓ problem and solution

**6.** What natural disasters occur in your area? What kind of research do you think scientists are doing to help lessen the future impact of these events?

Answers will vary.

**125**

---

**1.** Classify the following statements as **T** if a statement is true or **F** if a statement is false.

F No one needs to forage for food today, but some people do it for fun anyway.

T For most of human history, hunting and gathering was the primary way humans got their food.

F Be sure to gather all of the edible plants growing in an area, because it will encourage more plants to grow back and replace the ones you took.

F If you decide to try foraging yourself, the most important rule is to make sure you forage on public property.

F Most of the plants growing in a wild environment will be highly toxic, so it is vital to have a field guide on hand.

**2.** Write a one-sentence summary for each paragraph in the text.

1. Hunting and gathering is an important part of human history.

2. Hunting and gathering is not a necessity today, but many people do it for fun.

3. Wild plants grow all over the place, but it is important to know which ones are safe to eat.

4. The most important first step to becoming a forager is to learn from someone who is experienced.

5. Be sure to forage only in places where it is allowed.

6. Do not take more than you need.

7. Learn which plants are deadly.

8. Refer to a cookbook to know how to prepare wild foods.

**3.** What evidence does the author provide to show that early humans were successful hunters and gatherers? Humans would not be here today if hunting and gathering was not a successful way to survive.

**4.** Which statement best summarizes the author's point of view? Place a checkmark on the line of the best answer.

_____ Once humans developed agriculture, the need to hunt and gather food became obsolete.

✓ Gathering wild edible plants is a fun and rewarding hobby that also has some risks, so it is important to learn about foraging before trying it out yourself.

_____ Poisonous plants and edible plants look familiar, so it is important to purchase a field guide.

_____ Public land is usually open to foraging, but you need to be sure there are no additional rules about protected plants.

**127**

# Answer Key

1. Identify the order of events by writing 1–8 on the lines.

    **7** Jackson finds a blackberry bush.

    **3** Jackson and Uncle Louis listen to the deer crunching through leaves.

    **6** Uncle Louis explains that the green husks contain walnuts.

    **8** Jackson decides to make blackberry jam for his mom's birthday.

    **4** Uncle Louis finds a patch of fireweed.

    **2** Uncle Louis motions for Jackson to stop.

    **1** Uncle Louis sees a deer on the trail.

    **5** Jackson tastes a fireweed flower.

2. Is this story an example of realistic fiction or fantasy? Explain your answer.

    Realistic fiction, because the plot and all the story elements could happen in real life.

3. Do you think Uncle Louis lives near Jackson and sees him often, or does he live in another place and the two don't see each other often? How do you know?

    Uncle Louis lives somewhere else and only visits from time to time. The author states that he is only there for a weekend visit.

4. What is the conflict in this story? How is the conflict resolved? The conflict is that Jackson does not know what present to give his mom for her birthday. The conflict is resolved when Jackson finds the blackberry bush and decides to make her jam.

5. What gift will Uncle Louis give his sister for her birthday? Uncle Louis's gift is to use the wild plants to make food for the party.

6. Do you think Jackson's mom will like his gift? Why or why not?

    Answers will vary. Possible answer: She will like the gift, because it will be made by Louis and is a thoughtful gift.

7. Do you have a relative you like to spend time with? What do you do together?

    Answers will vary.

**129**

# Notes

# Notes

**Notes**